意外と言えない英単語・英熟語

「回転すし」を英語で言えますか?

デイビッド・セイン

アスコム

はじめに

> 「回転すしを
> 英語で言えますか？」

こう質問すると、
ほとんどの日本人が

> 「kaiten-sushi」

と答えます。
でも、残念ながら、
これは間違いです。

答えは、

> 「conveyor-belt sushi」

そう言わないと
よっぽど日本に詳しい外国人以外には
伝わりません。

ほかにも、
言えそうで言えない単語や熟語、
いろいろありますよね。

たとえば、これは言えますか?

- **肉じゃが**
- **おみくじ**
- **あやとり**
- **駅伝**
- **コンセント**
- **ぬいぐるみ**
- **リップクリーム**
- **はし置き**
- **五十肩**

はじめに

2020年には東京で
オリンピックが開かれることもあり、
海外から来る方がどんどん増えていきます。
海外旅行をしなくても
英語を使う機会が増えているんです。

みなさんのまわりでも、
　・歩いていたら道を聞かれた、
　・行きつけの料理屋に外国人が来ていた、
　・外国人が隣に引っ越してきた、
など、
外国人とコミュニケーションをとる
機会がきっとあるはずです。

本書では、会話によく出てくる単語や、
覚えたら言いたくなるような単語を
たっぷりと約1700語収録しました。

単語・熟語は英会話の基礎の基礎。
これが言えないと、
相手に自分の思いが伝わりません。
ぜひ、本書を活用して、
英会話を楽しみましょう！

David A. Thayne

目次

CHAPTER 1 食に関する言葉 007

すし／洋食／ファストフード
お弁当／居酒屋／中国料理
和食1／和食2／うどん、そば、ラーメン
朝食／ご飯／魚、貝／肉／野菜、豆
果物／カフェ／駄菓子／和菓子
洋菓子／味、食感

CHAPTER 2 健康に関する言葉 049

病院／体調、病気、ケガ1
体調、病気、ケガ2／体調、病気、ケガ3
薬／ダイエット／身体
マッサージ、整体／ジム／歯
目／つめ、手／足／お腹

CHAPTER 3 人に関する言葉 079

人の描写／表情／子育て
おもちゃ、遊び／親せき
世間話／結婚／ケンカ／心／友達
着物／アクセサリー、くつ／洋服

目次

CHAPTER 4 趣味、レジャーに関する言葉 … 107

本1／本2／テレビ／電話／SNS／インターネット
映画／文具／お祭り／日本の行事／祝日／手紙1
手紙2／美術／けいこ、趣味／スポーツ
音楽、楽器／ゲーム／旅行／遊園地／写真

CHAPTER 5 知識に関する言葉 … 151

国語／算数／理科／社会／政治、経済
新聞／日本文化／和小物
天気／暑さ、寒さ／哺乳動物
虫／鳥／色／植物／スケジュール

CHAPTER 6 家に関する言葉 … 185

掃除／洗濯／料理1／料理2／料理3／食器
化粧、洗顔／トイレ／車、バイク、自転車
電気／宅配便／寝具／生活／家

CHAPTER 7 街に関する言葉 … 215

お店／コンビニ／買い物／電車／駅、切符
タクシー、バス／信号、道路／学校関連
公共施設／神社、仏閣／銀行

CHAPTER 1

食に関する言葉
Food

食べることに関する話題は、世界共通で盛り上がります。肉や魚、野菜といった食材の名前はもちろん、和食や洋食、中国料理などで出てくる料理名や、洋菓子や和菓子の名前をまとめました。

Food

INDEX

- すし
- 洋食
- ファストフード
- お弁当
- 居酒屋
- 中国料理
- 和食 1
- 和食 2
- うどん、そば、ラーメン
- 朝食
- ご飯
- 魚、貝
- 肉
- 野菜、豆
- 果物
- カフェ
- 駄菓子
- 和菓子
- 洋菓子
- 味、食感

CHAPTER 1 食に関する言葉
すし

1. ☑ 回転すし
2. ☑ (回らない) すし屋
3. ☑ ネタ
4. ☑ シャリ
5. ☑ 酢飯
6. ☑ わさび
7. ☑ ガリ
8. ☑ 軍艦巻き
9. ☑ まぐろ
10. ☑ いか
11. ☑ いくら
12. ☑ 穴子
13. ☑ 鉄火巻
14. ☑ かっぱ巻き
15. ☑ かんぴょう巻き
16. ☑ ちらしすし

CHAPTER 1. 食に関する言葉 | すし

CHAPTER 1 Food
Sushi

1. conveyor-belt sushi
2. sushi bar
3. sushi topping
4. sushi rice
5. vinegared rice
6. wasabi mustard
7. gari ginger
8. warship roll
9. tuna
10. squid
11. salmon roe
12. conger
13. tuna roll
14. cucumber roll
15. gourd roll
16. vinegared rice with toppings

CHAPTER 1 食に関する言葉
洋食

1. ☑ ハンバーグ
2. ☑ オムライス
3. ☑ オムレツ
4. ☑ エビフライ
5. ☑ カニクリームコロッケ
6. ☑ コース料理
7. ☑ シーザーサラダ
8. ☑ タルタルソース
9. ☑ コンソメスープ
10. ☑ ビーフシチュー
11. ☑ ソテー
12. ☑ メンチカツ
13. ☑ ミートソーススパゲッティ
14. ☑ ポテトグラタン
15. ☑ チキンドリア
16. ☑ 鮭のムニエル

CHAPTER 1. 食に関する言葉 | 洋食

CHAPTER 1
Food
Western food

1. hamburger
2. omelet rice
3. omelet
4. fried shrimp
5. crab cream croquette
6. course cuisine
7. Caesar salad
8. tartar sauce
9. consomme soup
10. beef stew
11. saute
12. mince cutlet
13. meat sauce spaghetti
14. potato gratin
15. chicken doria
16. breaded and butter-fried salmon steak

CHAPTER 1 食に関する言葉
ファストフード

1. ☑ ハンバーガー
2. ☑ 牛丼
3. ☑ ホットドッグ
4. ☑ ハンバーガーセット
5. ☑ 店内で食べる
6. ☑ 持ち帰る
7. ☑ 食券を買う
8. ☑ コーラ
9. ☑ フライドポテト
10. ☑ フライドチキン
11. ☑ シェイク
12. ☑ ナゲット
13. ☑ 宅配ピザ
14. ☑ サンドイッチ
15. ☑ ソフトクリーム
16. ☑ コールスロー

CHAPTER 1. 食に関する言葉 | ファストフード

CHAPTER 1 — Food
Fast food

1. hamburger
2. beef bowl
3. hot dog
4. hamburger combo
5. eat in the restraunt
6. to go
7. buy a meal ticket
8. coke
9. French fries
10. fried chicken
11. shake
12. nuggets
13. home-delivered pizza
14. sandwich
15. soft-serve ice cream
16. coleslaw

CHAPTER 1 お弁当
食に関する言葉

1. ☑ 弁当を作る
2. ☑ 弁当を詰める
3. ☑ コンビニ弁当
4. ☑ 駅弁
5. ☑ 手製の弁当
6. ☑ 愛妻弁当
7. ☑ 日の丸弁当
8. ☑ 宅配弁当
9. ☑ 日替わり弁当
10. ☑ のり弁
11. ☑ シャケ弁
12. ☑ 弁当箱
13. ☑ いなりすし
14. ☑ 太巻きすし
15. ☑ 賞味期限
16. ☑ 割りばし

CHAPTER 1. 食に関する言葉｜お弁当

CHAPTER 1 Food
Lunch box

1. make a lunch box
2. put something in a lunch box
3. convenience-store lunch box
4. train-station lunch box
5. handmade lunch box
6. lunch box made by my wife
7. lunch box with only rice and umeboshi
8. home-delivered lunch (set)
9. the lunch box of the day
10. seaweed lunch box
11. salmon lunch box
12. lunch box
13. rice in a deep-fried tofu pocket
14. large sushi roll
15. sell by (date)
16. disposable chopsticks

CHAPTER 1 食に関する言葉
居酒屋

1. 居酒屋でコンパする
2. 居酒屋で打ち上げをする
3. 居酒屋で飲み明かす
4. 居酒屋をハシゴする
5. 割り勘にする
6. 全国チェーン店の居酒屋
7. 朝まで営業している居酒屋
8. おつまみ
9. 枝豆
10. 焼き鳥
11. から揚げ
12. ビール
13. 日本酒
14. 焼酎
15. ハイボール
16. サワー

CHAPTER 1. 食に関する言葉｜居酒屋

Food
Bars and taverns

1. have a party at a bar
2. have a wrap-up party
3. drink the night away at a bar
4. go barhopping
5. pay separate
6. national chain of bars
7. all-night bar
8. snacks
9. green soybeans
10. yakitori chicken
11. fried chicken
12. beer
13. sake
14. distilled spirits
15. highball
16. (gin) sour

CHAPTER 1 食に関する言葉
中国料理

1. ☐ エビチリ
2. ☐ 麻婆豆腐
3. ☐ 酢豚
4. ☐ ふかひれ
5. ☐ 小籠包
6. ☐ 春巻き
7. ☐ 北京ダック
8. ☐ かた焼きそば
9. ☐ 冷やし中華
10. ☐ ピータン
11. ☐ ザーサイ
12. ☐ エビシュウマイ
13. ☐ 餃子
14. ☐ 杏仁豆腐
15. ☐ ウーロン茶
16. ☐ プーアル茶

CHAPTER 1. 食に関する言葉｜中国料理

CHAPTER 1 Food
Chinese food

1. shrimp in chili sauce
2. Sichuan style bean curd
3. sweet and sour pork
4. shark fin
5. Chinese dumplings
6. spring roll
7. Peking duck
8. Hong Kong style crispy chow mein
9. cold Chinese noodles
10. thousand-year-old egg
11. Sichuan vegetable pickles
12. shrimp dumplings
13. gyoza dumplings
14. almond jelly
15. oolong tea
16. pu'er tea

020

CHAPTER 1 和食 1
食に関する言葉

1. ☑ 天ぷら
2. ☑ しゃぶしゃぶ
3. ☑ すき焼き
4. ☑ 湯どうふ
5. ☑ ちゃんこ鍋
6. ☑ てっちり
7. ☑ 懐石料理
8. ☑ 精進料理
9. ☑ 丼物
10. ☑ 茶わん蒸し
11. ☑ 親子丼
12. ☑ 味噌汁
13. ☑ お吸い物
14. ☑ 刺身
15. ☑ 焼き魚
16. ☑ 煮魚

CHAPTER 1. 食に関する言葉 | 和食 1

CHAPTER 1
Food
Japanese food 1

1. tempura
2. shabu-shabu meat
3. sukiyaki
4. tofu hot pot
5. sumo wrestler hot pot
6. blowfish hot pot
7. tea-ceremony dishes
8. vegetarian cuisine
9. rice bowl dishes
10. steamed egg custard
11. chicken and egg rice bowl
12. miso soup
13. clear soup
14. sashimi
15. grilled fish
16. boiled fish

CHAPTER 1 食に関する言葉
和食 2

1. 野菜炒め
2. おでん
3. 定食
4. 冷奴
5. 厚揚げ
6. 油揚げ
7. 酢の物
8. 煮物
9. しょうが焼き
10. きんぴら
11. 肉じゃが
12. 漬物
13. かまぼこ
14. お好み焼き
15. たこ焼き
16. もんじゃ焼き

CHAPTER 1. 食に関する言葉 | 和食 2

CHAPTER 1 Food
Japanese food 2

1. stir-fried vegetables
2. oden hot pot
3. set meal
4. cold tofu
5. deep-fried tofu
6. deep-fried thin tofu
7. marinated cucumber and wakame salad
8. simmered dish
9. fried ginger pork
10. sauteed and simmered vegetables
11. simmered meat and potatoes
12. pickles
13. kamaboko fish cake
14. okonomiyaki pancake
15. octopus dumplings
16. monjayaki pancake

CHAPTER 1 食に関する言葉
うどん、そば、ラーメン

1. ざるそば
2. きつねそば
3. たぬきうどん
4. 鍋焼きうどん
5. だし
6. 薬味
7. かき揚げ
8. そば湯
9. そうめん
10. きしめん
11. しょうゆラーメン
12. 味噌ラーメン
13. とんこつラーメン
14. つけ麺
15. レンゲ
16. なると

CHAPTER 1. 食に関する言葉 | うどん、そば、ラーメン

CHAPTER 1
Food
Udon, soba, ramen

1. cold zarusoba noodles
2. soba with deep-fried tofu
3. noodles with bits of deep-fried tempura batter
4. udon served in a pot with broth
5. soup stock
6. condiment
7. mixed tempura
8. soba cooking water
9. thin wheat noodles
10. noodles made in flat strips
11. soy sauce ramen
12. miso ramen
13. pork ramen
14. dipping noodles
15. ramen spoon
16. sliced fish cake

CHAPTER 1 食に関する言葉
朝食

1. ☐ バイキング形式
2. ☐ トースト
3. ☐ マーガリン
4. ☐ オレンジマーマレード
5. ☐ 納豆
6. ☐ ほうれんそうのおひたし
7. ☐ 生卵
8. ☐ 目玉焼き
9. ☐ 半熟卵
10. ☐ ゆで卵
11. ☐ 炒り卵
12. ☐ ウインナー
13. ☐ クロワッサン
14. ☐ ロールパン
15. ☐ シリアル
16. ☐ グラノーラ

CHAPTER 1. 食に関する言葉｜朝食

CHAPTER 1 Food
Breakfast

1. all-you-can-eat style
2. toast
3. margarine
4. (orange) marmalade
5. natto
6. boiled spinach
7. raw egg
8. fried egg
9. soft-boiled eggs
10. boiled egg
11. scrambled egg
12. wiener
13. croissant
14. (bread) bun
15. (breakfast) cereal
16. granola

028

CHAPTER 1 食に関する言葉
ご飯

1. ☑ お米を研ぐ
2. ☑ お米を水に浸す
3. ☑ ご飯を炊く
4. ☑ ご飯が炊き上がる
5. ☑ ご飯を保温する
6. ☑ ご飯をお代わりする
7. ☑ ご飯が喉に詰まる
8. ☑ ご飯を握る
9. ☑ 炊きたてのご飯
10. ☑ 炊き込みご飯
11. ☑ お粥
12. ☑ お茶漬
13. ☑ ふりかけ
14. ☑ おにぎり
15. ☑ おこげ
16. ☑ チャーハン

CHAPTER 1.　食に関する言葉｜ご飯

CHAPTER 1　Food
Rice

1. rinse the rice
2. soak the rice in water
3. let the rice steam
4. the rice is done
5. keep the rice warm
6. have another serving of rice
7. have rice caught in my throat
8. form the rice into balls
9. freshly cooked rice
10. seasoned rice
11. rice porridge
12. rice mixed with tea
13. seasoning for sprinkling on rice
14. rice ball
15. burned okoge rice
16. fried rice

CHAPTER 1 食に関する言葉
魚、貝

1. あじ
2. いわし
3. さんま
4. 明太子
5. たこ
6. ふぐ
7. すっぽん
8. ちりめんじゃこ
9. さけ
10. うなぎ
11. あさり
12. しじみ
13. さば
14. 甘えび
15. かに
16. たい

CHAPTER 1.　食に関する言葉｜魚、貝

CHAPTER 1
Food
Fish, shellfish

1. horse mackerel
2. true sardine
3. Pacific saury
4. seasoned cod roe
5. octopus
6. blowfish
7. soft-shelled turtle
8. boiled and dried young sardine
9. salmon
10. eel
11. clam
12. freshwater clam
13. mackerel
14. pink shrimp
15. crab
16. red sea bream

CHAPTER 1 食に関する言葉
肉

1. ☐ 牛肉
2. ☐ 豚肉
3. ☐ 鶏肉
4. ☐ 羊肉
5. ☐ 肉をぶつ切りにする
6. ☐ 肉を細切りにする
7. ☐ 肉を角切りにする
8. ☐ 肉を焼く
9. ☐ 肉を塩で焼く
10. ☐ 肉をステーキにする
11. ☐ ひき肉
12. ☐ あいびき肉
13. ☐ 赤身
14. ☐ 脂身
15. ☐ 霜降り肉
16. ☐ 熟成肉

CHAPTER 1. 食に関する言葉｜肉

CHAPTER 1 Food
Meat

1. beef
2. pork
3. chicken
4. mutton
5. cut the meat into chunks
6. cut the meat into strips
7. cut the meat into cubes
8. fry the meat
9. grill the meat with salt
10. cook the meat as a steak
11. minced meat
12. ground beef and pork
13. lean meat
14. fat
15. marbled beef
16. aged meat

CHAPTER 1 食に関する言葉
野菜、豆

1. ☑ さつまいも
2. ☑ 大根
3. ☑ にら
4. ☑ ねぎ
5. ☑ ピーマン
6. ☑ もやし
7. ☑ 大豆
8. ☑ そら豆
9. ☑ みょうが
10. ☑ なす
11. ☑ セロリ
12. ☑ 白菜
13. ☑ きゅうり
14. ☑ ほうれんそう
15. ☑ かぶ
16. ☑ きんとき豆

CHAPTER 1. 食に関する言葉 | 野菜、豆

CHAPTER 1 Food
Vegetables, beans

1. sweet potato
2. radish
3. Chinese chive
4. leek
5. green pepper
6. bean sprouts
7. soybean
8. broad bean
9. Japanese ginger
10. eggplant
11. celery
12. Chinese cabbage
13. cucumber
14. spinach
15. turnip
16. red kidney bean

CHAPTER 1 食に関する言葉
果物

1. ☐ キウイ
2. ☐ すいか
3. ☐ くり
4. ☐ かき
5. ☐ すもも
6. ☐ さくらんぼ
7. ☐ みかん
8. ☐ 日向夏

9. ☐ きんかん
10. ☐ なし
11. ☐ 白桃
12. ☐ いちご
13. ☐ ぶどう
14. ☐ びわ
15. ☐ メロン
16. ☐ あんず

CHAPTER 1. 食に関する言葉 | 果物

CHAPTER 1 Food
Fruits

1. kiwi
2. watermelon
3. chestnut
4. persimmon
5. Japanese plum
6. cherry
7. Japanese tangerine
8. hyuga summer orange
9. kumquat
10. Japanese pear
11. white peach
12. strawberry
13. grape
14. loquat
15. melon
16. apricot

CHAPTER 1 カフェ
食に関する言葉

1. ☑ コーヒー
2. ☑ 紅茶
3. ☑ ミルクティー
4. ☑ コーヒーフレッシュ
5. ☑ カフェラテ
6. ☑ 抹茶
7. ☑ ココア
8. ☑ アメリカンコーヒー
9. ☑ 濃いコーヒー
10. ☑ ホットケーキ
11. ☑ ワッフル
12. ☑ フルーツパフェ
13. ☑ フレンチトースト
14. ☑ メロンソーダ
15. ☑ コーラフロート
16. ☑ コーヒーゼリー

CHAPTER 1. 食に関する言葉 | カフェ

Food
Cafe

1. coffee
2. black tea
3. tea with milk
4. cream
5. coffee latte
6. matcha green tea
7. hot chocolate
8. regular coffee
9. strong coffee
10. pancake
11. waffle
12. fruit parfait
13. French toast
14. green soda
15. coke float
16. coffee jelly

CHAPTER 1 食に関する言葉
駄菓子

1. ☑ 駄菓子屋
2. ☑ ラムネ
3. ☑ ラムネ菓子
4. ☑ グミ
5. ☑ 酢いか
6. ☑ スナック菓子
7. ☑ ポテトチップ
8. ☑ 板チョコ
9. ☑ あめ
10. ☑ 麩菓子
11. ☑ フーセンガム
12. ☑ マシュマロ
13. ☑ ぽん菓子
14. ☑ えびせん
15. ☑ あられ
16. ☑ ビスケット

CHAPTER 1. 食に関する言葉 | 駄菓子

CHAPTER 1 Food
Candy and snacks

1. mom-and-pop candy store
2. lemon soda
3. soda-drop candy
4. gummy candy
5. vinegar squid
6. junk food
7. potato chips
8. chocolate bar
9. candy
10. bran confectionery
11. bubble gum
12. marshmallow
13. puffed rice
14. shrimp flavored snack
15. bite-sized rice-crack snack
16. biscuit cookie

CHAPTER 1 　和菓子

食に関する言葉

1. まんじゅう
2. 大福
3. ようかん
4. せんべい
5. たい焼き
6. どら焼き
7. ぎゅうひ
8. カステラ
9. おはぎ
10. 白玉
11. あんみつ
12. もなか
13. 寒天
14. おしるこ
15. かき氷
16. らくがん

CHAPTER 1. 食に関する言葉 | 和菓子

CHAPTER 1
Food
Japanese confectionery

1. steamed bread
2. daifuku rice cake
3. yokan bean jelly
4. senbei cracker
5. fish-shaped pancake filled with bean jam
6. dorayaki snack
7. gyuhi rice cake
8. castella cake
9. bean cake
10. shiratama riceball
11. anmitsu syrup
12. bean paste sandwich
13. agar
14. sweet red-bean soup with rice-flour dumplings
15. snow cone
16. embossed sugar candy

CHAPTER 1 食に関する言葉
洋菓子

1. ☐ クッキー
2. ☐ チョコレート
3. ☐ マドレーヌ
4. ☐ モンブラン
5. ☐ ロールケーキ
6. ☐ ショートケーキ
7. ☐ シフォンケーキ
8. ☐ タルト
9. ☐ シュークリーム
10. ☐ エクレア
11. ☐ マカロン
12. ☐ ミルフィーユ
13. ☐ ミルクレープ
14. ☐ チョコレートムース
15. ☐ スフレ
16. ☐ プリン

CHAPTER 1. 食に関する言葉｜洋菓子

CHAPTER 1 Food
Pastries

1. cookie
2. chocolate
3. madeleine
4. Mont Blanc
5. Swiss roll
6. shortcake
7. chiffon cake
8. tart
9. cream puff
10. eclair
11. macaroon
12. mille-feuille pastry
13. mille-crepe
14. chocolate mousse
15. souffle
16. pudding

CHAPTER 1 食に関する言葉
味、食感

1. ☑ 辛い
2. ☑ 苦い
3. ☑ 甘い
4. ☑ すっぱい
5. ☑ しょっぱい
6. ☑ 濃い
7. ☑ 薄い
8. ☑ もちもち
9. ☑ ふわふわ
10. ☑ ぼそぼそ
11. ☑ さらさら
12. ☑ どろっとした
13. ☑ かたい
14. ☑ やわらかい
15. ☑ おいしい
16. ☑ まずい

CHAPTER 1. 食に関する言葉｜味、食感

CHAPTER 1
Food
Taste, texture

1. hot
2. bitter
3. sweet
4. sour
5. salty
6. heavy/strong (tasting)
7. light (tasting)
8. chewy
9. fluffy
10. dry and tasteless
11. refreshing
12. gooey
13. hard
14. soft
15. delicious
16. bad tasting

CHAPTER 2

健康に関する言葉
Health

体調、病気、病院、体のことなどは、知らないといざという時に困ってしまいます。そんな時、症状について説明できるように、健康に関する単語・熟語をまとめました。ジムや整体に関する言葉も紹介します。

Health

INDEX

- ●病院
- ●体調、病気、ケガ1
- ●体調、病気、ケガ2
- ●体調、病気、ケガ3
- ●薬
- ●ダイエット
- ●身体
- ●マッサージ、整体
- ●ジム
- ●歯
- ●目
- ●つめ、手
- ●足
- ●お腹

CHAPTER 2 健康に関する言葉
病院

1. ☐ 病院に通う
2. ☐ 病院に診察券を出す
3. ☐ 病院で診てもらう
4. ☐ 入院する
5. ☐ 退院する
6. ☐ 病院に見舞いに行く
7. ☐ 内科
8. ☐ 外科
9. ☐ 小児科
10. ☐ 皮膚科
11. ☐ 産婦人科
12. ☐ 精神科
13. ☐ 歯医者
14. ☐ 看護師
15. ☐ 担当医
16. ☐ かかりつけの医者

CHAPTER 2. 健康に関する言葉｜病院

CHAPTER 2
Health
Hospitals

1. ☑ visit the hospital
2. ☑ show my patient registration card to the hospital
3. ☑ go see a doctor
4. ☑ enter a hospital
5. ☑ get released from the hospital
6. ☑ see someone in a hospital
7. ☑ internal medicine
8. ☑ surgery
9. ☑ pediatrics
10. ☑ dermatology
11. ☑ department of obstetrics and gynecology
12. ☑ psychiatry
13. ☑ dentist
14. ☑ nurse
15. ☑ attending physician
16. ☑ family doctor

CHAPTER 2 健康に関する言葉
体調、病気、ケガ1

1. ☑ だるい
2. ☑ 便秘
3. ☑ 熱っぽい
4. ☑ むくみ
5. ☑ 吐き気がする
6. ☑ 頭痛
7. ☑ 胃痛
8. ☑ 寝違える
9. ☑ 花粉症
10. ☑ 鼻づまり
11. ☑ 鼻水
12. ☑ 鼻血
13. ☑ 二日酔い
14. ☑ 喉の痛み
15. ☑ 肩こり
16. ☑ 口内炎

CHAPTER 2. 健康に関する言葉｜体調、病気、ケガ 1

CHAPTER 2
Health
Physical condition, illness, injuries 1

1. languid
2. constipation
3. feverish
4. puffiness
5. feel like throwing up
6. headache
7. stomach pain
8. wake up with a cricked neck
9. hay fever
10. nasal congestion
11. snot
12. bloody nose
13. hangover
14. soar throat
15. stiff neck
16. canker sore

CHAPTER 2 健康に関する言葉
体調、病気、ケガ 2

1. ☐ 風邪
2. ☐ 膝痛
3. ☐ 腰痛
4. ☐ 骨折
5. ☐ 青あざ
6. ☐ 出血
7. ☐ 擦り傷
8. ☐ 打撲
9. ☐ 刺し傷
10. ☐ 切り傷
11. ☐ 水ぶくれ
12. ☐ こむらがえり
13. ☐ 五十肩
14. ☐ 魚の目
15. ☐ タコの目
16. ☐ 病気になる

CHAPTER 2.　健康に関する言葉｜体調、病気、ケガ 2

CHAPTER 2 — Health
Physical condition, illness, injuries 2

1. cold
2. knee pain
3. low back pain
4. fracture
5. bruise
6. bleeding
7. abrasion
8. black and blue
9. stab wound
10. cut
11. blister
12. cramp
13. frozen shoulder
14. corn
15. callus
16. get sick

CHAPTER 2 健康に関する言葉
体調、病気、ケガ 3

1. ☑ 病気が重い
2. ☑ 病気で寝込む
3. ☑ 病気をうつす
4. ☑ 病気を診断する
5. ☑ 病気が軽くなる
6. ☑ 病気を克服する
7. ☑ 病気を口実にする
8. ☑ 病気を嘆く
9. ☑ 重い病気
10. ☑ 不治の病
11. ☑ 遺伝性の病気
12. ☑ 先天性の病気
13. ☑ 伝染性の病気
14. ☑ 病気がち
15. ☑ 病気を予防する
16. ☑ 病気の潜伏期間

CHAPTER 2. 健康に関する言葉｜体調、病気、ケガ 3

CHAPTER 2
Health
Physical condition, illness, injuries 3

1. be really sick
2. be sick in bed
3. give someone my illness
4. diagnose
5. get a little better
6. get over my illness
7. use my sickness as an excuse
8. get depressed about having an illness
9. serious illness
10. incurable disease
11. hereditary disease
12. congenital disease
13. contagious disease
14. prone to sickness
15. keep from getting sick
16. the latent period

CHAPTER 2 健康に関する言葉
薬

1. ☑ 薬を常用する
2. ☑ 薬が効く／効かない
3. ☑ カプセル状の薬
4. ☑ 粉末の薬
5. ☑ 錠剤
6. ☑ 風邪薬
7. ☑ 頭痛薬
8. ☑ 胃腸薬
9. ☑ 目薬
10. ☑ 酔い止め
11. ☑ 下剤
12. ☑ ビタミン剤
13. ☑ 抗生物質
14. ☑ 痛み止め
15. ☑ 点鼻薬
16. ☑ 漢方薬

CHAPTER 2. 健康に関する言葉 | 薬

CHAPTER 2 Health
Medicine

1. take medicine regularly
2. be effective/ineffective
3. capsules
4. powder medicine
5. pill
6. cold medicine
7. headache medicine
8. stomach medicine
9. eye drops
10. motion-sickness medicine
11. laxative
12. vitamin supplement
13. antibiotic
14. pain killer
15. nasal drops
16. herbal medicine

CHAPTER 2 健康に関する言葉
ダイエット

1. ☑ ダイエット器具
2. ☑ ダイエット食品
3. ☑ リバウンド
4. ☑ 体重
5. ☑ 体重管理
6. ☑ やせる
7. ☑ 太る
8. ☑ カロリー
9. ☑ 糖質
10. ☑ カロリーゼロ
11. ☑ 体脂肪
12. ☑ 腹筋
13. ☑ 背筋
14. ☑ 運動
15. ☑ 食事制限
16. ☑ 低糖質食

CHAPTER 2. 健康に関する言葉 | ダイエット

CHAPTER 2 Health
Diet

1. ☑ diet equipment
2. ☑ diet food
3. ☑ rebound
4. ☑ body weight
5. ☑ weight management
6. ☑ lose weight
7. ☑ gain weight
8. ☑ calorie
9. ☑ carbohydrate
10. ☑ zero calorie
11. ☑ body fat
12. ☑ abs (abdominal muscles の略)
13. ☑ back muscles
14. ☑ exercise
15. ☑ restricted diet
16. ☑ low-carbohydrate diet

CHAPTER 2 健康に関する言葉
身体

1. ☑ ひざ
2. ☑ ひじ
3. ☑ まゆげ
4. ☑ 口ひげ
5. ☑ あごひげ
6. ☑ 腰
7. ☑ ふくらはぎ
8. ☑ ふともも
9. ☑ かかと
10. ☑ つま先
11. ☑ 指先
12. ☑ つめ
13. ☑ 関節
14. ☑ 背骨
15. ☑ おへそ
16. ☑ 筋肉

CHAPTER 2. 健康に関する言葉｜身体

CHAPTER 2 Health
Body

1. knee
2. elbow
3. eyebrow
4. mustache
5. beard
6. waist
7. calf
8. thigh
9. heel
10. toe
11. fingertip
12. nail
13. joint
14. spine
15. navel
16. muscle

CHAPTER 2 健康に関する言葉
マッサージ、整体

1. ☑ もむ
2. ☑ 叩く
3. ☑ 押す
4. ☑ 整体師
5. ☑ 施術
6. ☑ 足裏マッサージ
7. ☑ 足湯
8. ☑ 整体
9. ☑ はり
10. ☑ お灸
11. ☑ つぼ
12. ☑ こり
13. ☑ ストレッチ
14. ☑ 30分コース
15. ☑ デトックス
16. ☑ 全身マッサージ

CHAPTER 2. 健康に関する言葉 | マッサージ、整体

CHAPTER 2 Health
Massage, bodywork

1. massage
2. pound
3. push
4. bodywork therapist
5. treatment
6. foot massage
7. foot bath
8. bodywork
9. acupuncture
10. moxibustion
11. acupuncture point
12. stiffness
13. stretch
14. 30 minute course
15. detox (detoxification)
16. full-body massage

CHAPTER 2　ジム

健康に関する言葉

1. ランニングマシーン
2. サイクリングマシーン
3. バーベル
4. ダンベル
5. 筋トレ
6. 鍛える
7. 走る
8. ダンベルをあげる
9. プール
10. 更衣室
11. サウナ
12. ヨガ
13. バランスボール
14. 個人トレーナー
15. フリーウェイト
16. 体重計

CHAPTER 2. 健康に関する言葉 | ジム

CHAPTER 2 Health
Gym

1. treadmill
2. exercise bike
3. barbell
4. dumbbell
5. muscle training
6. train
7. run
8. raise the dumbbell
9. pool
10. locker room
11. sauna
12. yoga
13. exercise ball
14. personal trainer
15. free weights
16. weight machine

CHAPTER 2 健康に関する言葉
歯

1. ☐ 歯が抜ける
2. ☐ 歯を磨く
3. ☐ 歯ぎしりする
4. ☐ 虫歯になる
5. ☐ 虫歯が痛む
6. ☐ 虫歯を治療する
7. ☐ 金歯
8. ☐ 入れ歯
9. ☐ 前歯
10. ☐ 糸切り歯
11. ☐ 奥歯
12. ☐ 親知らず
13. ☐ 乳歯
14. ☐ 永久歯
15. ☐ 歯磨き紛
16. ☐ 歯ブラシ

CHAPTER 2. 健康に関する言葉 | 歯

CHAPTER 2
Health
Teeth

1. tooth falls out
2. brush my teeth
3. grind my teeth
4. get a cavity
5. have a cavity that hurts
6. treat a cavity
7. crowned tooth
8. false tooth
9. front tooth
10. canine tooth
11. molar
12. wisdom tooth
13. baby tooth
14. permanent tooth
15. toothpaste
16. toothbrush

CHAPTER 2 健康に関する言葉

目

1. ☐ 目をつぶる
2. ☐ 目を細くする
3. ☐ 目を休める
4. ☐ 視力が落ちる
5. ☐ 目がかすむ
6. ☐ 視力を検査する
7. ☐ 近視の
8. ☐ 遠視の
9. ☐ 乱視
10. ☐ 老眼の
11. ☐ 充血した
12. ☐ 白内障
13. ☐ メガネをかける
14. ☐ メガネがくもる
15. ☐ 使い捨てのコンタクト
16. ☐ コンタクトをつける

CHAPTER 2. 健康に関する言葉 | 目

CHAPTER 2 Health
Eyes

1. close my eyes
2. narrow my eyes
3. rest my eyes
4. eyes go bad
5. have blurry eyes
6. have my eyes checked
7. nearsighted
8. farsighted
9. astigmatism
10. old sight
11. bloodshot
12. cataract
13. put on glasses
14. glasses get foggy
15. disposable contact lens
16. put in contacts

CHAPTER 2 健康に関する言葉
つめ、手

1. ☑ つめを切る
2. ☑ つめをそろえる
3. ☑ つめが伸びる
4. ☑ つめを磨く
5. ☑ つめにマニキュアを塗る
6. ☑ つめを手入れする
7. ☑ 手を叩く
8. ☑ 手をつなぐ
9. ☑ 手を挙げる
10. ☑ 手を差し出す
11. ☑ 手をつかむ
12. ☑ 手をふりほどく
13. ☑ しわだらけの手
14. ☑ 荒れた手
15. ☑ ひび割れた手
16. ☑ ハンドクリーム

CHAPTER 2. 健康に関する言葉 | つめ、手

CHAPTER 2
Health
Fingernails, hands

1. cut my fingernails
2. trim my fingernails
3. get long
4. polish my fingernails
5. paint my fingernails
6. do my fingernails
7. clap my hands
8. hold hands
9. raise my hand
10. hold out my hand
11. grasp my hand
12. pull my hand free
13. wrinkled hands
14. chapped hands
15. cracked hands
16. hand cream

CHAPTER 2 足
健康に関する言葉

1. ☐ 足をばたばたさせる
2. ☐ 足を踏みならす
3. ☐ 足を棒にする
4. ☐ 足を骨折する
5. ☐ 足首を捻挫する
6. ☐ 足がつる
7. ☐ 足をくすぐる
8. ☐ 引き締まった足
9. ☐ むくんだ足
10. ☐ 足の裏
11. ☐ あぐらをかく
12. ☐ 足を休める
13. ☐ 足をさする
14. ☐ 足をもむ
15. ☐ 太い足
16. ☐ 細い足

CHAPTER 2. 健康に関する言葉 | 足

CHAPTER 2 Health
Legs

1. kick and struggle
2. stomp my feet
3. walk myself lame
4. break a leg
5. sprain an ankle
6. get a cramp in my leg
7. tickle my feet
8. firm legs
9. swollen legs
10. soles of my feet
11. sit cross-legged
12. rest my feet
13. rub my leg
14. massage my feet
15. fat legs
16. slender legs

CHAPTER 2　健康に関する言葉
お腹

1. ☐ お腹を空かす
2. ☐ お腹いっぱいになる
3. ☐ お腹をこわす
4. ☐ お腹を下す
5. ☐ ウエストが太くなる
6. ☐ ウエストが細くなる
7. ☐ ウエストがたるむ
8. ☐ 引き締まった腹
9. ☐ 三段腹
10. ☐ ビール腹
11. ☐ 中年太り
12. ☐ 腹八分目
13. ☐ お腹が出る
14. ☐ お腹がへこむ
15. ☐ お腹の肉をつまむ
16. ☐ お腹の贅肉

CHAPTER 2. 健康に関する言葉｜お腹

CHAPTER 2
Health
Stomach

1. ☑ be hungry
2. ☑ be full
3. ☑ have a stomachache
4. ☑ have diarrhea
5. ☑ get heavy around my waist
6. ☑ get thin around my waist
7. ☑ get flabby around my waist
8. ☑ flat stomach
9. ☑ three spare tires
10. ☑ beer belly
11. ☑ middle-age spread
12. ☑ not completely full
13. ☑ get a bulge around my stomach
14. ☑ get skinny
15. ☑ grab the fat around my waist
16. ☑ excess fat around my stomach

CHAPTER 3

人に関する言葉
People

人の性格を表す言葉や、感情を伝える言葉、家族や親せき、友人といった人間関係を描写する言葉を紹介します。結婚や子育て、ケンカに関する言葉もまとめています。

People

INDEX

- 人の描写
- 表情
- 子育て
- おもちゃ、遊び
- 親せき
- 世間話
- 結婚
- ケンカ
- 心
- 友達
- 着物
- アクセサリー、くつ
- 洋服

CHAPTER 3 人に関する言葉
人の描写

1. ☑ ひねくれた
2. ☑ おっとりした
3. ☑ 神経質な
4. ☑ さっぱりした
5. ☑ 狭量な
6. ☑ 引っ込み思案な
7. ☑ 強引な
8. ☑ 目立ちたがりな
9. ☑ 美人
10. ☑ きれい
11. ☑ かわいい
12. ☑ かっこいい
13. ☑ イケメン
14. ☑ ブサイク
15. ☑ 明るい
16. ☑ 暗い

CHAPTER 3. 人に関する言葉 | 人の描写

CHAPTER 3 People
Human characteristics

1. ☑ cynical
2. ☑ gentle
3. ☑ nervous
4. ☑ open
5. ☑ narrow-minded
6. ☑ shy
7. ☑ pushy
8. ☑ boastful
9. ☑ beauty
10. ☑ beautiful
11. ☑ cute
12. ☑ cool
13. ☑ good looking
14. ☑ ugly
15. ☑ happy
16. ☑ gloomy

CHAPTER 3 人に関する言葉
表情

1. ☑ 泣く
2. ☑ 笑う
3. ☑ はにかんだ
4. ☑ 困った
5. ☑ 怒った
6. ☑ がっかりした
7. ☑ 悲しそうな
8. ☑ いらいらした
9. ☑ 驚く
10. ☑ 困惑
11. ☑ 嫌悪
12. ☑ 苦笑
13. ☑ うんざり
14. ☑ 恐怖
15. ☑ 表情豊か
16. ☑ 無表情

CHAPTER 3. 人に関する言葉 | 表情

CHAPTER 3 People
Expressing emotions

1. cry
2. smile
3. shy
4. embarrassed
5. anger
6. feel disappointed
7. sad
8. impatient
9. surprised
10. puzzled
11. dislike
12. bitter smile
13. fed up
14. fear
15. expressive
16. expressionless face

CHAPTER 3 人に関する言葉
子育て

1. ☑ 子どもを育てる
2. ☑ 子どもをほめる
3. ☑ 子どもを叱る
4. ☑ 子どもをなだめる
5. ☑ いたずらっ子
6. ☑ 泣き虫な子
7. ☑ お転婆な子
8. ☑ わんぱくな子
9. ☑ 反抗期
10. ☑ 子守
11. ☑ 留守番
12. ☑ おつかい
13. ☑ 離乳食
14. ☑ 哺乳瓶
15. ☑ おむつ
16. ☑ 指しゃぶり

CHAPTER 3. People — Children

1. raise a child	9. rebellious phase
2. praise a child	10. baby-sitter
3. scold a child	11. stay at home by yourself
4. calm a child	12. errand
5. mischievous child	13. baby food
6. crybaby	14. baby bottle
7. tomboy	15. diaper
8. naughty child	16. finger sucking

CHAPTER 3 人に関する言葉
おもちゃ、あそび

1. ☐ あやとり
2. ☐ 積木
3. ☐ 木製のおもちゃ
4. ☐ 人形
5. ☐ ミニカー
6. ☐ なわとび
7. ☐ 鬼ごっこ
8. ☐ かくれんぼ
9. ☐ 木馬
10. ☐ おままごと
11. ☐ はいはい
12. ☐ よちよち歩き
13. ☐ いないいないばあ
14. ☐ じゃんけんぽん
15. ☐ プラモデル
16. ☐ ぬいぐるみ

CHAPTER 3. 人に関する言葉 | おもちゃ、あそび

CHAPTER 3
People
Toys, plays

1. string figure
2. toy blocks
3. wooden toys
4. doll
5. miniature car
6. jump rope
7. play tag
8. hide-and-seek
9. wooden horse
10. play house
11. crawling
12. toddling
13. peek-a-boo
14. paper, rock, scissors
15. plastic model
16. stuffed toy

CHAPTER 3 人に関する言葉
親せき

1. ☑ いとこ
2. ☑ はとこ
3. ☑ 孫
4. ☑ 祖父母
5. ☑ 娘
6. ☑ 長女、次女
7. ☑ 三人兄弟
8. ☑ 姉妹
9. ☑ 兄、弟
10. ☑ 双子
11. ☑ 姪／甥
12. ☑ 叔父
13. ☑ 叔母
14. ☑ 夫婦
15. ☑ 姑／舅
16. ☑ 末っ子

CHAPTER 3. 人に関する言葉｜親せき

CHAPTER 3 People
Relatives

1. cousin
2. second cousin
3. grandchild
4. grandparent
5. daughter
6. eldest daughter, second daughter
7. three brothers
8. sisters
9. (older) brother, (younger) brother
10. twins
11. niece/nephew
12. uncle
13. aunt
14. husband and wife
15. mother-in-law/father-in-law
16. youngest child

CHAPTER 3　人に関する言葉
世間話

1. ☑ うわさする

2. ☑ うわさを流す

3. ☑ うわさをささやく

4. ☑ うわさを伝える

5. ☑ うわさを信じる

6. ☑ うわさを疑う

7. ☑ うわさを耳にする

8. ☑ うわさに踊らされる

9. ☑ うわさをあおる

10. ☑ うわさを恐れる

11. ☑ うわさを苦にする

12. ☑ とんでもないうわさ

13. ☑ 根拠のないうわさ

14. ☑ 知れ渡っているうわさ

15. ☑ 誰かに聞いたうわさ

16. ☑ うわさをやめる

CHAPTER 3. 人に関する言葉 | 世間話

CHAPTER 3　People
Small talk

1. gossip
2. spread a rumor
3. whisper a rumor
4. repeat a rumor
5. believe a rumor
6. doubt a rumor
7. hear a rumor
8. be affected by a rumor
9. help spread a rumor
10. fear a rumor
11. be worried by a rumor
12. ridiculous rumor
13. groundless rumor
14. widely known rumor
15. rumor heard from someone
16. end a rumor

CHAPTER 3 人に関する言葉
結婚

1. ☐ 結婚を夢見る
2. ☐ 結婚を焦る
3. ☐ 結婚を決意する
4. ☐ 結婚を切り出す
5. ☐ 結婚を取りやめる
6. ☐ 結婚を喜ぶ
7. ☐ 結婚を延期する
8. ☐ 結婚をためらう
9. ☐ 結婚を祝福する
10. ☐ 初婚
11. ☐ 再婚
12. ☐ 見合い結婚
13. ☐ 二重結婚
14. ☐ 事実婚
15. ☐ でき婚
16. ☐ 成田離婚

CHAPTER 3. 人に関する言葉 | 結婚

CHAPTER 3
People
Marriage

1. dream of getting married
2. be in a hurry to get married
3. make up one's mind to marry someone
4. bring up the subject of marriage
5. break off an engagement
6. be happy with a marriage
7. put off marriage
8. hesitate to marry someone
9. give one's blessing to someone's marriage
10. first marriage
11. second marriage
12. arranged marriage
13. bigamy
14. common-law marriage
15. shotgun marriage
16. honeymoon divorce

CHAPTER 3 人に関する言葉
ケンカ

1. ☑ ケンカする
2. ☑ ケンカを売る
3. ☑ ケンカを買う
4. ☑ ケンカをやめる
5. ☑ ケンカをやめて仲直りする
6. ☑ ささいなことでケンカする
7. ☑ ケンカを仲裁する
8. ☑ ケンカをけしかける
9. ☑ ケンカをたしなめる
10. ☑ 痴話ゲンカ
11. ☑ 夫婦ゲンカ
12. ☑ 兄弟ゲンカ
13. ☑ 親子ゲンカ
14. ☑ 口ゲンカ
15. ☑ 激しいケンカ
16. ☑ 1対1のケンカ

CHAPTER 3. People

Fighting

1. (get in a) fight
2. pick a fight
3. accept someone's challenge
4. stop fighting
5. stop fighting and make up
6. fight over nothing
7. mediate a fight
8. start a fight
9. scold someone for fighting
10. lover's quarrel
11. marital quarrel
12. sibling quarrel
13. family dispute
14. argument
15. violent fight
16. one-on-one fight

CHAPTER 3 人に関する言葉
心

1. ☑ 心を込める
2. ☑ 心を配る
3. ☑ 心をときめかす
4. ☑ 心を躍らせる
5. ☑ あわれみの心
6. ☑ 狭量な心
7. ☑ 虚栄心
8. ☑ 猜疑心
9. ☑ 出来心
10. ☑ 下心
11. ☑ 警戒心
12. ☑ 心ここにあらず
13. ☑ 心を入れ替える
14. ☑ 心が通じ合う
15. ☑ 心を触れ合わせる
16. ☑ 心を静める

CHAPTER 3. 人に関する言葉 | 心

CHAPTER 3
People
Psychology

1. pour one's heart into something
2. pay attention to someone
3. flutter with excitement
4. get excited about
5. merciful heart
6. narrow mind
7. self-conceit
8. suspicion
9. impulse
10. secret intention
11. caution
12. but not in spirit
13. become a new person
14. understand each other
15. establish a rapport
16. calm down

CHAPTER 3 人に関する言葉
友達

1. ☑ 友達をつくる
2. ☑ 友達を集める
3. ☑ 友達ができない
4. ☑ 友達と親しくする
5. ☑ 毎日のように友達と遊びまわる
6. ☑ 友達をからかう
7. ☑ 友達をいじめる
8. ☑ 親友
9. ☑ 大親友
10. ☑ 悪友
11. ☑ 級友
12. ☑ 旧友
13. ☑ 幼友達
14. ☑ 飲み友達
15. ☑ 遊び友達
16. ☑ メル友

CHAPTER 3. 人に関する言葉｜友達

CHAPTER 3 People
Friends

1. make a friend
2. gather my friends
3. not be able to make friends
4. be good friends with someone
5. go out with my friends almost every day
6. make fun of my friend
7. bully my friend
8. close friend
9. really close friend
10. bad friend
11. classmate
12. old friend
13. childhood friend
14. drinking friend
15. good buddy
16. e-mail friend

CHAPTER 3 人に関する言葉
着物

1. ☑ 浴衣
2. ☑ 下駄
3. ☑ 草履
4. ☑ 帯
5. ☑ 袖
6. ☑ 着付け
7. ☑ 足袋
8. ☑ 振袖
9. ☑ 訪問着
10. ☑ 肌じゅばん
11. ☑ はかま
12. ☑ 羽織
13. ☑ 作務衣
14. ☑ 甚平
15. ☑ はんてん
16. ☑ 帯留

CHAPTER 3. 人に関する言葉 | 着物

CHAPTER 3
People
Kimono

1. yukata robe
2. geta sandals
3. straw sandals
4. obi belt
5. kimono sleeve
6. put on a kimono
7. tabi stockings
8. long-sleeved kimono
9. visiting kimono
10. kimono underwear
11. hakama skirt
12. haori coat
13. monk's working clothes
14. summertime casual wear
15. hanten coat
16. sash clip

CHAPTER 3 　人に関する言葉
アクセサリー、くつ

1. ☑ ピアス

2. ☑ イヤリング

3. ☑ ペンダント

4. ☑ 指輪

5. ☑ 腕時計

6. ☑ バングル

7. ☑ ブローチ

8. ☑ アンクル

9. ☑ ハイヒール

10. ☑ スニーカー

11. ☑ サンダル

12. ☑ ミュール

13. ☑ ブーツ

14. ☑ ハイヒール

15. ☑ ビーチサンダル

16. ☑ くつひも

CHAPTER 3. 人に関する言葉｜アクセサリー、くつ

CHAPTER 3
People
Accessories, shoes

1. pierced earring
2. earring
3. pendant
4. ring
5. wrist watch
6. bangle
7. brooch
8. anklet
9. high-heeled shoes
10. sneakers
11. sandals
12. mule shoes
13. boots
14. leather shoes
15. flip-flops
16. shoelace

CHAPTER 3 人に関する言葉
洋服

1. ☑ ジャケット
2. ☑ シャツ
3. ☑ パンツ
4. ☑ スーツ
5. ☑ スカート
6. ☑ プリーツスカート
7. ☑ くつした
8. ☑ タイツ
9. ☑ セーター
10. ☑ カーディガン
11. ☑ カットソー
12. ☑ Tシャツ
13. ☑ ダッフルコート
14. ☑ トレンチコート
15. ☑ レインコート
16. ☑ ワンピース

CHAPTER 3. 人に関する言葉 | 洋服

CHAPTER 3
People
Clothes

1. jacket
2. shirt
3. pants
4. suit
5. skirt
6. pleated skirt
7. socks
8. tights
9. sweater
10. cardigan
11. cut sew
12. T-shirt
13. duffle coat
14. trench coat
15. raincoat
16. one-piece dress

CHAPTER 4

趣味・レジャーに関する言葉

Leisure

本や映画、旅行やスポーツなどに関する言葉、電話や手紙、SNSなどで使われる言葉など、趣味や余暇の時間に関する言葉を集めました。

Leisure

INDEX

- ●本 1
- ●本 2
- ●テレビ
- ●電話
- ●SNS
- ●インターネット
- ●映画
- ●文具
- ●お祭り
- ●日本の行事
- ●祝日
- ●手紙 1
- ●手紙 2
- ●美術
- ●けいこ、趣味
- ●スポーツ
- ●音楽、楽器
- ●ゲーム
- ●旅行
- ●遊園地
- ●写真

CHAPTER 4 趣味・レジャーに関する言葉
本1

1. ☑ 本を読み聞かせる
2. ☑ 本を読破する
3. ☑ 本を音読する
4. ☑ 本を黙読する
5. ☑ 本を積む
6. ☑ 本をのぞき込む
7. ☑ 本を勧める
8. ☑ 役に立たない本
9. ☑ 一気に読める本
10. ☑ ビジネス書
11. ☑ マンガ
12. ☑ 写真集
13. ☑ 絵本
14. ☑ 文庫
15. ☑ ハードカバー
16. ☑ 新書

CHAPTER 4. 趣味・レジャーに関する言葉 | 本 1

CHAPTER 4
Leisure
Books 1

1. ☑ read a book to someone
2. ☑ read through a book
3. ☑ read a book out loud
4. ☑ read a book to oneself
5. ☑ stack the books
6. ☑ peek at a book
7. ☑ recommend a book
8. ☑ worthless book
9. ☑ a book that can be read in one sitting
10. ☑ business book
11. ☑ comic
12. ☑ photo collection
13. ☑ picture book
14. ☑ library
15. ☑ hardcover
16. ☑ shinsho size book

CHAPTER 4 本2

趣味・レジャーに関する言葉

1. ☑ ライトノベル
2. ☑ ホラー
3. ☑ ガイドブック
4. ☑ 参考書
5. ☑ 図鑑
6. ☑ 辞書
7. ☑ ゲーム攻略本
8. ☑ レシピ本
9. ☑ 推理小説
10. ☑ 歴史本
11. ☑ 雑誌
12. ☑ 小説
13. ☑ 詩集
14. ☑ ファッション誌
15. ☑ フィクション
16. ☑ ノンフィクション

CHAPTER 4. 趣味・レジャーに関する言葉 | 本 2

CHAPTER 4
Leisure
Books 2

1. ☑ light novel
2. ☑ horror
3. ☑ guidebook
4. ☑ reference book
5. ☑ picture book
6. ☑ dictionary
7. ☑ game strategy book
8. ☑ recipe book
9. ☑ mystery
10. ☑ history book
11. ☑ magazine
12. ☑ novel
13. ☑ collection of poems
14. ☑ fashion magazine
15. ☑ fiction
16. ☑ nonfiction

CHAPTER 4 テレビ

趣味・レジャーに関する言葉

1. ☑ アニメ
2. ☑ ドラマ
3. ☑ 昼ドラ
4. ☑ 連ドラ
5. ☑ クイズ番組
6. ☑ 天気予報
7. ☑ 深夜番組
8. ☑ 子ども向け番組
9. ☑ バラエティ
10. ☑ ドキュメンタリー
11. ☑ ニュース番組
12. ☑ 通販番組
13. ☑ CM
14. ☑ 再放送
15. ☑ 裏番組
16. ☑ 生放送

CHAPTER 4. 趣味・レジャーに関する言葉 | テレビ

CHAPTER 4
Leisure
Television

1. anime
2. drama
3. mid-day drama
4. drama series
5. quiz show
6. weather forecast
7. late-night show
8. children's program
9. variety show
10. documentary
11. news program
12. TV shopping program
13. commercial
14. rebroadcast
15. a program on a different channel at the same time
16. live broadcast

CHAPTER 4 趣味・レジャーに関する言葉
電話

1. ☑ 電話をかける
2. ☑ 電話に出る
3. ☑ 電話を保留にする
4. ☑ 電話に番号を登録する
5. ☑ 電話の着信音を変更する
6. ☑ 携帯電話を充電する
7. ☑ 携帯電話の充電が切れる
8. ☑ 携帯電話をマナーモードにする
9. ☑ 携帯電話のマナーモードを解除する
10. ☑ 折り畳み式の携帯電話
11. ☑ ガラケー
12. ☑ スマホ
13. ☑ 電波がいい/悪い
14. ☑ 回線が速い
15. ☑ 留守電
16. ☑ 電話を切る

CHAPTER 4. 趣味・レジャーに関する言葉 | 電話

CHAPTER 4 Leisure
Telephones

1. call someone
2. answer a phone
3. put someone on hold
4. add someone's number to my phone
5. change the ring tone on a phone
6. recharge a mobile phone
7. run out of power
8. put a mobile phone on manner mode
9. release the manner mode on a mobile phone
10. foldable mobile phone
11. old (fashioned) phone
12. smartphone
13. strong/weak signal
14. fast line
15. answering machine
16. end a call

CHAPTER 4　SNS

趣味・レジャーに関する言葉

1. ☐ バズる
2. ☐ つぶやく
3. ☐ シェアする
4. ☐ いいね！
5. ☐ 投稿する
6. ☐ 削除する
7. ☐ 返信する
8. ☐ 検索する
9. ☐ 写真をアップする
10. ☐ タグをつける
11. ☐ 顔文字／絵文字
12. ☐ メッセージを送る／受け取る
13. ☐ 更新する
14. ☐ 友達申請
15. ☐ 既読スルー
16. ☐ 既読

CHAPTER 4. 趣味・レジャーに関する言葉 | SNS

CHAPTER 4
Leisure
SNSs

1. ☑ go viral
2. ☑ tweet
3. ☑ share
4. ☑ Like!
5. ☑ post
6. ☑ remove
7. ☑ respond
8. ☑ search for
9. ☑ upload photos
10. ☑ tag (a photo)
11. ☑ emoticons/ pictogram
12. ☑ send/receive a (text) message
13. ☑ update
14. ☑ friend someone
15. ☑ read through
16. ☑ already read

CHAPTER 4 インターネット
趣味・レジャーに関する言葉

- 1 ☑ メールを送信する
- 2 ☑ メールを受信する
- 3 ☑ メールに返信する
- 4 ☑ ネットサーフィン
- 5 ☑ ウイルスに感染する
- 6 ☑ アンチウイルスソフト
- 7 ☑ 動画
- 8 ☑ 画像
- 9 ☑ ニュースサイト
- 10 ☑ 検索エンジン
- 11 ☑ スパムメール
- 12 ☑ ノートパソコン
- 13 ☑ インターネットを活用する
- 14 ☑ インターネットを使いこなす
- 15 ☑ インターネットの接続設定を行う
- 16 ☑ ネットオークションに参加する

CHAPTER 4. 趣味・レジャーに関する言葉 | インターネット

CHAPTER 4 Leisure
Internet

1. send a message
2. receive a message
3. reply to an (e-mail) message
4. Internet surfing
5. infected with a virus
6. antivirus software
7. animation
8. image
9. news site
10. search engine
11. spam mail
12. laptop PC
13. use the Internet
14. be skilled at using the Internet
15. set up an Internet connection
16. participate in an Internet auction

CHAPTER 4 趣味・レジャーに関する言葉
映画

1. ☑ 映画を観る
2. ☑ 映画に感動する
3. ☑ 映画俳優
4. ☑ 映画監督
5. ☑ 映画字幕
6. ☑ アクション映画
7. ☑ 恋愛映画
8. ☑ 子ども向け映画
9. ☑ アニメ映画
10. ☑ サスペンス映画
11. ☑ ホラー映画
12. ☑ 冒険映画
13. ☑ SF映画
14. ☑ 名作映画
15. ☑ 大作映画
16. ☑ 大ヒット映画

CHAPTER 4. 趣味・レジャーに関する言葉 | 映画

CHAPTER 4 Leisure
Movies

1. see a movie (映画館で), watch a movie (家で)
2. be touched by a movie
3. movie actor
4. movie director
5. movie subtitles
6. action movie
7. love-story movie
8. kids movie
9. animated movie
10. suspense movie
11. horror movie
12. adventure movie
13. science-fiction movie
14. masterpiece movie
15. major movie
16. mega-hit movie

CHAPTER 4 趣味・レジャーに関する言葉
文具

1. ☑ 万年筆
2. ☑ ボールペン
3. ☑ シャーペン
4. ☑ 鉛筆
5. ☑ 鉛筆削り
6. ☑ 消しゴム
7. ☑ 赤ペン
8. ☑ サインペン
9. ☑ 油性マジック
10. ☑ 多色ボールペン
11. ☑ はさみ
12. ☑ 色鉛筆
13. ☑ カッター
14. ☑ ホチキス
15. ☑ 定規
16. ☑ 消せるボールペン

CHAPTER 4. 趣味・レジャーに関する言葉 | 文具

CHAPTER 4
Leisure
Stationary

1. fountain pen
2. ballpoint pen
3. mechanical pencil
4. pencil
5. sharpener
6. eraser
7. red pen
8. felt-tip pen
9. permanent marker
10. multicolor ballpoint pen
11. scissors
12. colored pencil
13. cutter
14. stapler
15. ruler
16. erasable ballpoint pen

CHAPTER 4　趣味・レジャーに関する言葉
お祭り

1. ☑ 夏祭り
2. ☑ 雪まつり
3. ☑ 屋台
4. ☑ 金魚すくい
5. ☑ りんごあめ
6. ☑ ソースせんべい
7. ☑ 盆踊り
8. ☑ チョコバナナ
9. ☑ わたあめ
10. ☑ 射的
11. ☑ ヨーヨー
12. ☑ おめん
13. ☑ おみこし
14. ☑ 阿波踊り
15. ☑ 縁日
16. ☑ 花火

CHAPTER 4. 趣味・レジャーに関する言葉 | お祭り

CHAPTER 4　Leisure
Festivals

1. summer festival
2. snow festival
3. stall
4. goldfish scooping
5. candied apple
6. sauce rice cracker
7. bon festival dance
8. chocolate banana
9. cotton candy
10. shooting
11. yo-yo
12. mask
13. portable shrine
14. awa dance
15. festival day
16. fireworks

CHAPTER 4　趣味・レジャーに関する言葉
日本の行事

1
☑ 初詣

2
☑ おとしだま

3
☑ 豆まき

4
☑ ひなまつり

5
☑ ひな人形

6
☑ こいのぼり

7
☑ 衣がえ

8
☑ 海開き

9
☑ 山開き

10
☑ お盆

11
☑ お墓参り

12
☑ 十五夜

13
☑ お月見

14
☑ 紅葉狩り

15
☑ 年越しそば

16
☑ 除夜の鐘

CHAPTER 4. 趣味・レジャーに関する言葉 | 日本の行事

CHAPTER 4
Leisure
Japanese events

1. ☑ New Year's visit to a shrine
2. ☑ New Year's gift
3. ☑ bean-throwing
4. ☑ Girl's Day
5. ☑ hina doll
6. ☑ carp streamer
7. ☑ wardrobe switch
8. ☑ beach opening ceremony
9. ☑ mountain opening ceremony
10. ☑ obon
11. ☑ grave visit
12. ☑ full moon festival
13. ☑ moon-viewing
14. ☑ maple-viewing
15. ☑ soba noodles on New Year's Eve
16. ☑ New Year's bells

CHAPTER 4 趣味・レジャーに関する言葉
祝日

1. ☑ 元日
2. ☑ 建国記念日
3. ☑ 憲法記念日
4. ☑ みどりの日
5. ☑ こどもの日
6. ☑ 海の日
7. ☑ 敬老の日
8. ☑ 秋分の日
9. ☑ 勤労感謝の日
10. ☑ 大晦日
11. ☑ 体育の日
12. ☑ 文化の日
13. ☑ 昭和の日
14. ☑ 天皇誕生日
15. ☑ 成人の日
16. ☑ 春分の日

CHAPTER 4. 趣味・レジャーに関する言葉 | 祝日

CHAPTER 4
Leisure
Public holidays

1. New Year's Day
2. National Foundation Day
3. Constitution Day
4. Greenery Day
5. Children's Day
6. Marine Day
7. Respect-for-the-Aged Day
8. Autumnal Equinox Day
9. Labor Thanksgiving Day
10. New Year's Eve
11. Sports Day
12. Culture Day
13. Showa Day
14. Emperor's Birthday
15. Coming-of-Age Day
16. Spring Equinox Day

CHAPTER 4　手紙 1
趣味・レジャーに関する言葉

1. ハガキ
2. 切手
3. 速達
4. 書留
5. 信書
6. 現金書留
7. 年賀状
8. 暑中見舞い
9. 寒中見舞い
10. 絵ハガキ
11. 便せん
12. 封筒
13. 定型郵便
14. 定型外郵便
15. 応募する
16. アンケートハガキ

CHAPTER 4. 趣味・レジャーに関する言葉 | 手紙 1

CHAPTER 4 Leisure
Letters 1

1. postcard
2. stamp
3. express delivery (mail)
4. registered (mail)
5. confidential correspondence
6. cash registration
7. New Year's card
8. summer greeting card
9. winter greeting card
10. picture postcard
11. letter paper
12. envelope
13. fixed-rate mail
14. irregular-sized mail
15. apply for something
16. questionnaire postcard

CHAPTER 4 趣味・レジャーに関する言葉
手紙 2

1. ☑ 往復ハガキ
2. ☑ お礼状
3. ☑ バースデーカード
4. ☑ クリスマスカード
5. ☑ ポスト
6. ☑ 郵便受け
7. ☑ 小包
8. ☑ 郵便番号
9. ☑ 住所
10. ☑ 宛名
11. ☑ 差出人
12. ☑ 手紙を書く
13. ☑ 手紙を送る
14. ☑ 手紙に切手を貼る
15. ☑ 郵便料金
16. ☑ 手紙をもらう

CHAPTER 4. 趣味・レジャーに関する言葉 | 手紙 2

CHAPTER 4
Leisure
Letters 2

1. return postcard
2. thank-you letter
3. birthday card
4. Christmas card
5. post
6. mailbox
7. parcel
8. postal code
9. street address
10. address
11. sender
12. write a letter
13. send a letter
14. put a stamp on a letter
15. postage
16. get a letter

CHAPTER 4 趣味・レジャーに関する言葉
美術

1. ☑ 絵を描く
2. ☑ 絵を描き上げる
3. ☑ 絵を飾る
4. ☑ 絵を鑑賞する
5. ☑ 絵に見とれる
6. ☑ 上手な絵
7. ☑ 油絵
8. ☑ パステル画
9. ☑ 鉛筆画
10. ☑ 水彩画
11. ☑ 水墨画
12. ☑ 有名な絵
13. ☑ 抽象的な絵
14. ☑ 印象派の絵
15. ☑ 見るものの心を打つ絵
16. ☑ 美術館

CHAPTER 4. 趣味・レジャーに関する言葉 | 美術

CHAPTER 4　Leisure
Art

1. draw a picture
2. finish drawing a picture
3. hang up a painting
4. look at paintings
5. be charmed by a painting
6. well-done painting
7. oil painting
8. pastel painting
9. pencil drawing
10. watercolor painting
11. Indian ink painting
12. famous painting
13. abstract painting
14. impressionist painting
15. breathtaking painting
16. museum

CHAPTER 4 けいこ、趣味

趣味・レジャーに関する言葉

1. ☑ 英会話教室
2. ☑ 料理教室
3. ☑ お菓子作り
4. ☑ マナー講座
5. ☑ 茶道
6. ☑ 華道
7. ☑ 書道
8. ☑ 資格
9. ☑ ワインソムリエ
10. ☑ ダンス
11. ☑ 編み物
12. ☑ 裁縫
13. ☑ コスプレ
14. ☑ 園芸
15. ☑ 登山
16. ☑ 食べ歩き

CHAPTER 4. 趣味・レジャーに関する言葉 | けいこ、趣味

CHAPTER 4
Leisure
Lessons, Hobbies

1. English conversation school
2. cooking class
3. pastry making
4. etiquette lesson
5. tea ceremony
6. Japanese flower arrangement
7. calligraphy
8. qualification
9. wine sommelier
10. dance
11. knitting
12. sewing
13. cosplay
14. gardening
15. mountain climbing
16. eating at restaurants

CHAPTER 4 スポーツ

趣味・レジャーに関する言葉

1. ☑ 空手
2. ☑ 柔道
3. ☑ 合気道
4. ☑ 体操
5. ☑ 相撲
6. ☑ 硬式テニス
7. ☑ 軟式テニス
8. ☑ 陸上
9. ☑ 長距離
10. ☑ 短距離
11. ☑ 駅伝
12. ☑ 野球
13. ☑ スポーツで汗を流す
14. ☑ スポーツに打ち込む
15. ☑ スポーツを究める
16. ☑ プロのスポーツ選手になる

CHAPTER 4. 趣味・レジャーに関する言葉 | スポーツ

CHAPTER 4 Leisure
Sports

1. karate
2. judo
3. aikido
4. gymnastics
5. sumo
6. tennis
7. soft tennis
8. land
9. long-distance running
10. short-distance running
11. relay road race
12. baseball
13. do sports
14. be absorbed in a sport
15. excel in sports
16. become a professional

CHAPTER 4 趣味・レジャーに関する言葉
音楽、楽器

1. ☑ 洋楽
2. ☑ 邦楽
3. ☑ ロック
4. ☑ クラシック
5. ☑ ジャズ
6. ☑ 演歌
7. ☑ サントラ
8. ☑ 楽譜
9. ☑ ト音記号
10. ☑ ヘ音記号
11. ☑ 音符
12. ☑ 和音
13. ☑ 吹奏楽
14. ☑ 合唱
15. ☑ 歌詞
16. ☑ 伴奏

CHAPTER 4. 趣味・レジャーに関する言葉 | 音楽、楽器

CHAPTER 4
Leisure
Music, Musical instruments

1. Western music
2. Japanese music
3. rock
4. classical
5. jazz
6. traditional ballad
7. sound-track
8. (musical) score
9. treble clef
10. bass clef
11. (musical) note
12. chord
13. wind (instrument) music
14. chorus
15. lyrics, words of a song
16. accompaniment

CHAPTER 4 　趣味・レジャーに関する言葉
ゲーム

1. ☑ ゲームソフト
2. ☑ アクションゲーム
3. ☑ ロールプレイングゲーム
4. ☑ オセロ
5. ☑ マージャン
6. ☑ 将棋
7. ☑ 囲碁
8. ☑ チェス
9. ☑ 人生ゲーム
10. ☑ 七並べ
11. ☑ ババ抜き
12. ☑ じゃんけん
13. ☑ 神経衰弱
14. ☑ ゲームセンター
15. ☑ UFOキャッチャー
16. ☑ プリクラ

CHAPTER 4. 趣味・レジャーに関する言葉 | ゲーム

CHAPTER 4
Leisure
Games

1. game software
2. action game
3. role-playing game
4. Othello
5. mah-jongg
6. Japanese chess
7. (play) go
8. (play) chess
9. The Game of Life
10. sevens
11. old maid
12. rock-paper-scissors
13. nervous breakdown
14. game arcade
15. crane game
16. photo booth picture

CHAPTER 4 旅行

趣味・レジャーに関する言葉

- [ ] 1 旅行に二人きりで出かける
- [ ] 2 ふらりと旅行に出る
- [ ] 3 旅行から帰る
- [ ] 4 旅行を前倒しする
- [ ] 5 旅行先で病に倒れる
- [ ] 6 海外旅行
- [ ] 7 国内旅行
- [ ] 8 ヨーロッパ旅行
- [ ] 9 世界一周旅行
- [ ] 10 家族旅行
- [ ] 11 新婚旅行
- [ ] 12 卒業旅行
- [ ] 13 研修旅行
- [ ] 14 社員旅行
- [ ] 15 修学旅行
- [ ] 16 日帰り旅行

CHAPTER 4. 趣味・レジャーに関する言葉｜旅行

CHAPTER 4 Leisure
Travel

1. go on a trip alone with someone
2. go on a trip without a definite purpose
3. come back from a trip
4. move ahead my trip
5. get sick while traveling
6. overseas trip
7. domestic trip
8. trip to Europe
9. trip around the world
10. family trip
11. honeymoon
12. graduation trip
13. study tour
14. company trip
15. school trip
16. one-day trip

CHAPTER 4 遊園地

趣味・レジャーに関する言葉

1. ☑ 観覧車
2. ☑ ジェットコースター
3. ☑ お化け屋敷
4. ☑ メリーゴーランド
5. ☑ 年間パス
6. ☑ ヒーローショー
7. ☑ アトラクション
8. ☑ 絶叫マシーン
9. ☑ 年齢制限
10. ☑ 身長制限
11. ☑ フリーフォール
12. ☑ ティーカップ
13. ☑ 子どもの乗り物
14. ☑ 乗り物に乗る
15. ☑ 水遊び場
16. ☑ ウォータースライダー

CHAPTER 4. 趣味・レジャーに関する言葉 | 遊園地

CHAPTER 4 Leisure
Amusement park

1. Ferris wheel
2. roller coaster
3. haunted house
4. merry-go-round
5. annual pass
6. hero show
7. attraction
8. thrill ride
9. age limit
10. height restriction
11. free fall
12. teacup
13. kiddy ride
14. go on the rides
15. water park
16. water slide

CHAPTER 4 写真

趣味・レジャーに関する言葉

1. ☑ スナップ写真
2. ☑ 家族写真
3. ☑ お見合い写真
4. ☑ 卒業写真
5. ☑ 全身写真
6. ☑ 証明写真
7. ☑ カラー写真
8. ☑ モノクロ写真
9. ☑ 記念写真
10. ☑ 隠し撮りした写真
11. ☑ 証拠写真
12. ☑ 写真集
13. ☑ 写真を撮る
14. ☑ 写真を現像する
15. ☑ 写真を焼き増しする
16. ☑ 写真を保存する

CHAPTER 4. 趣味・レジャーに関する言葉 | 写真

CHAPTER 4 Leisure
Photography

1. snapshot
2. family portrait
3. photograph for a potential marriage partner
4. graduation portrait
5. full-body photograph
6. ID picture
7. colored photograph
8. black-and-white photograph
9. anniversary photograph
10. paparazzi photograph
11. photographic proof
12. photograph collection
13. take a picture
14. develop film
15. make copies of a photograph
16. store a photograph

CHAPTER 5

知識に関する言葉
Knowledge

日本人のほとんどがなかなか言えない、学校で習った科目や、鳥、動物、虫、色などの名称、そして、日本の和の文化など、知っていると会話が豊かになるような言葉をまとめました。

Knowledge

INDEX

- 国語
- 算数
- 理科
- 社会
- 政治、経済
- 新聞
- 日本文化
- 和小物

- 天気
- 暑さ、寒さ
- 哺乳動物
- 虫
- 鳥
- 色
- 植物
- スケジュール

CHAPTER 5 　知識に関する言葉
国語

1. ☑ 漢字
2. ☑ ひらがな
3. ☑ かたかな
4. ☑ 音読み
5. ☑ 訓読み
6. ☑ 主語
7. ☑ 述語
8. ☑ 修飾語
9. ☑ 敬語
10. ☑ ため口
11. ☑ 記号
12. ☑ ことわざ
13. ☑ 慣用句
14. ☑ 書き順
15. ☑ 名詞
16. ☑ 動詞

CHAPTER 5. 知識に関する言葉｜国語

CHAPTER 5
Knowledge
Language

1. Chinese character
2. hiragana writing
3. katakana writing
4. on reading
5. kun reading
6. subject
7. predicate
8. modifier
9. honorific
10. talk in a casual way
11. symbol
12. proverb
13. idiom
14. stroke order
15. noun
16. verb

CHAPTER 5 知識に関する言葉

算数

1. ☑ 足し算
2. ☑ 割り算
3. ☑ 掛け算
4. ☑ 引き算
5. ☑ 偶数
6. ☑ 奇数
7. ☑ 小数点
8. ☑ 九九
9. ☑ 素数
10. ☑ 最大公約数
11. ☑ 最小公倍数
12. ☑ 時速
13. ☑ 秒速
14. ☑ 正方形
15. ☑ 長方形
16. ☑ 円形

CHAPTER 5. 知識に関する言葉 | 算数

CHAPTER 5
Knowledge
Arithmetic

1. ☑ addition
2. ☑ division
3. ☑ multiplication
4. ☑ subtraction
5. ☑ even (number)
6. ☑ odd (number)
7. ☑ point
8. ☑ multiplication table
9. ☑ prime (number)
10. ☑ the greatest common divisor
11. ☑ the least common multiple
12. ☑ speed per hour
13. ☑ speed per second
14. ☑ square
15. ☑ rectangle
16. ☑ circle

CHAPTER 5 　知識に関する言葉
理科

1. ☑ アルコールランプ
2. ☑ ビーカー
3. ☑ フラスコ
4. ☑ スポイト
5. ☑ 温度計
6. ☑ リトマス紙
7. ☑ 酸性
8. ☑ 中性
9. ☑ アルカリ性
10. ☑ 液体
11. ☑ 気体
12. ☑ 固体
13. ☑ 草食動物
14. ☑ 肉食動物
15. ☑ 物理学
16. ☑ 生物学

CHAPTER 5. 知識に関する言葉｜理科

CHAPTER 5
Knowledge
Science

1. spirit lamp
2. beaker
3. flask
4. dropper
5. thermometer
6. litmus paper
7. acidity
8. neutral
9. alkaline
10. liquid
11. gas
12. solid
13. herbivore
14. carnivore
15. physics
16. biology

CHAPTER 5 社会
知識に関する言葉

1. ☑ 年号
2. ☑ 偉人
3. ☑ 埴輪
4. ☑ 青銅器
5. ☑ 古墳
6. ☑ 幕府
7. ☑ 武士
8. ☑ 一揆
9. ☑ 鎖国
10. ☑ 開国
11. ☑ 黒船
12. ☑ 明治維新
13. ☑ 黒船来航
14. ☑ 教育改革
15. ☑ 少子化
16. ☑ 高齢化

CHAPTER 5. 知識に関する言葉 | 社会

CHAPTER 5
Knowledge
Society

1. the name of an era
2. a great man
3. clay image
4. bronze ware
5. tomb
6. shogunate
7. samurai
8. riot
9. isolationism
10. opening of a country
11. black ships (from America)
12. Meiji Restoration
13. arrival of the black ships
14. education reform
15. declining birthrate
16. aging of society

CHAPTER 5 知識に関する言葉
政治、経済

1. ☑ 内閣
2. ☑ 選挙
3. ☑ 総理大臣
4. ☑ 大臣
5. ☑ 環境省
6. ☑ 文部科学省
7. ☑ 厚生労働省
8. ☑ 与党
9. ☑ 野党
10. ☑ 解散
11. ☑ 好景気
12. ☑ 不況
13. ☑ バブル
14. ☑ 円高
15. ☑ ドル安
16. ☑ 株価

CHAPTER 5. 知識に関する言葉｜政治、経済

CHAPTER 5
Knowledge
Politics, economics

1. ☑ cabinet
2. ☑ election
3. ☑ prime minister
4. ☑ minister
5. ☑ Ministry of the Environment
6. ☑ Ministry of Education, Culture, Sports, Science and Technology
7. ☑ Ministry of Health, Labour and Welfare
8. ☑ ruling party
9. ☑ opposition party
10. ☑ dissolution
11. ☑ booming economy
12. ☑ depression
13. ☑ bubble
14. ☑ strong yen
15. ☑ weak dollar
16. ☑ stock price

CHAPTER 5 知識に関する言葉
新聞

1. ☑ 新聞を購読する
2. ☑ 新聞を配達する
3. ☑ 新聞を束ねる
4. ☑ 新聞記事を切り抜く
5. ☑ 朝刊
6. ☑ 夕刊
7. ☑ 日曜版の新聞
8. ☑ スポーツ新聞
9. ☑ 経済新聞
10. ☑ テレビ欄
11. ☑ 社会面
12. ☑ 経済面
13. ☑ 地方版
14. ☑ 政治面
15. ☑ 1面
16. ☑ 広告面

CHAPTER 5. 知識に関する言葉 | 新聞

CHAPTER 5

Knowledge

Newspaper

1. subscribe to a newspaper
2. deliver a newspaper
3. bundle the newspapers
4. cut out a newspaper article
5. morning newspaper
6. evening newspaper
7. Sunday newspaper
8. sports newspaper
9. financial newspaper
10. the television guide in a newspaper
11. the society page
12. the financial page
13. the regional-news page
14. the politics page
15. the front page
16. advertisement page

CHAPTER 5 日本文化

知識に関する言葉

1. ☑ 能
2. ☑ 歌舞伎
3. ☑ 落語
4. ☑ 和歌
5. ☑ 俳句
6. ☑ 日本舞踊
7. ☑ 狂言
8. ☑ 民謡
9. ☑ 舞妓
10. ☑ 紅葉狩り
11. ☑ 花見
12. ☑ 獅子舞
13. ☑ 盆栽
14. ☑ ちんどんや
15. ☑ 浮世絵
16. ☑ 鳥獣戯画

CHAPTER 5. 知識に関する言葉｜日本文化

CHAPTER 5 Knowledge
Japanese culture

1. noh (drama)
2. kabuki (drama)
3. rakugo comic story
4. waka poem
5. haiku poem
6. classical Japanese dance
7. kyogen comedy
8. folk song
9. apprentice geisha
10. enjoy the autumn leaves
11. cherry-blossom viewing
12. lion dance
13. dwarf tree
14. chindonya street advertisers
15. Japanese woodblock prints
16. wildlife caricature

CHAPTER 5 知識に関する言葉
和小物

1. ☑ 巾着
2. ☑ 根付
3. ☑ 扇子
4. ☑ かんざし
5. ☑ こけし
6. ☑ がまぐち
7. ☑ 風鈴
8. ☑ 和傘
9. ☑ うちわ
10. ☑ 招き猫
11. ☑ まごの手
12. ☑ こま
13. ☑ ベーゴマ
14. ☑ かるた
15. ☑ 風呂敷
16. ☑ 折り紙

CHAPTER 5. 知識に関する言葉｜和小物

CHAPTER 5
Knowledge
Japanese accessories

1. ☑ purse
2. ☑ netsuke charm
3. ☑ folding fan
4. ☑ ornamental hairpin
5. ☑ kokeshi doll
6. ☑ coin purse
7. ☑ wind bell
8. ☑ Japanese umbrella
9. ☑ round fan
10. ☑ beckoning cat
11. ☑ back scratcher
12. ☑ (spinning) top
13. ☑ begoma spinning top
14. ☑ karuta cards
15. ☑ wrapping cloth
16. ☑ origami

CHAPTER 5 知識に関する言葉
天気

1. ☑ 晴れ
2. ☑ 快晴
3. ☑ くもり
4. ☑ 雨
5. ☑ 豪雨
6. ☑ 梅雨
7. ☑ 雷雨
8. ☑ 雪
9. ☑ 吹雪
10. ☑ 雷
11. ☑ にわか雨
12. ☑ みぞれ
13. ☑ じめじめ
14. ☑ 風が強い
15. ☑ 台風
16. ☑ 雪崩

CHAPTER 5. 知識に関する言葉｜天気

CHAPTER 5
Knowledge
Weather

1. nice weather
2. sunny weather
3. cloudiness
4. rain
5. heavy rain
6. rainy season
7. thunderstorm
8. snow
9. snowstorm
10. thunder
11. shower
12. sleet
13. damp and humid
14. strong wind
15. typhoon
16. avalanche

CHAPTER 5　知識に関する言葉
暑さ、寒さ

1. 暑さ/寒さがこたえる
2. 暑さ/寒さが増す
3. 暑さ/寒さが和らぐ
4. 暑さ/寒さに耐える
5. 暑さ/寒さに弱い
6. 暑さ/寒さを避ける
7. 暑さ/寒さをものともしない
8. 暑さ/寒さを防ぐ
9. 暑さが厳しい
10. 寒さが厳しい
11. 暑さでめまいがする
12. 寒さで手足がかじかむ
13. 寒さで足が冷える
14. 気温
15. 例年にない暑さ/寒さ
16. 例年並みの気温

CHAPTER 5. 知識に関する言葉｜暑さ、寒さ

CHAPTER 5
Knowledge
Heat and cold

1. the heat/cold gets to me
2. get hotter/colder
3. the heat/cold let up
4. endure the heat/cold
5. not take the heat/cold well
6. avoid the heat/cold
7. the heat/cold doesn't bother me at all
8. protect myself from the heat/cold
9. burning hot
10. freezing cold
11. be made dizzy by the temperature
12. be numb with cold
13. my legs get cold
14. temperature
15. hotter/colder than normal
16. average temperature

CHAPTER 5 知識に関する言葉
哺乳動物

1. ☑ キリン
2. ☑ カバ
3. ☑ サイ
4. ☑ ナマケモノ
5. ☑ シカ
6. ☑ アライグマ
7. ☑ イノシシ
8. ☑ ヤギ
9. ☑ キツネ
10. ☑ アザラシ
11. ☑ アシカ
12. ☑ モグラ
13. ☑ コウモリ
14. ☑ ロバ
15. ☑ タヌキ
16. ☑ リス

CHAPTER 5. 知識に関する言葉｜哺乳動物

CHAPTER 5
Knowledge
Mammals

1. giraffe
2. hippopotamus
3. rhinoceros
4. sloth
5. deer
6. raccoon
7. wild boar
8. goat
9. fox
10. seal
11. sea lion
12. mole
13. bat
14. donkey
15. raccoon dog
16. squirrel

CHAPTER 5 知識に関する言葉
虫

1. ☑ カブトムシ
2. ☑ クワガタ
3. ☑ アリ
4. ☑ ミミズ
5. ☑ ダンゴムシ
6. ☑ チョウチョ
7. ☑ セミ
8. ☑ トンボ
9. ☑ カマキリ
10. ☑ 蚊
11. ☑ テントウムシ
12. ☑ バッタ
13. ☑ クモ
14. ☑ アゲハチョウ
15. ☑ モンシロチョウ
16. ☑ ムカデ

CHAPTER 5. 知識に関する言葉 | 虫

CHAPTER 5
Knowledge
Insects

1. beetle
2. stag beetle
3. ant
4. earthworm
5. potato bug, pill bug
6. butterfly
7. cicada
8. dragonfly
9. praying mantis
10. mosquito
11. ladybug
12. grasshopper
13. spider
14. swallowtail butterfly
15. cabbage butterfly
16. centipede

CHAPTER 5 　知識に関する言葉

鳥

1. ☑ ニワトリ
2. ☑ ツバメ
3. ☑ ペンギン
4. ☑ ワシ
5. ☑ タカ
6. ☑ カラス
7. ☑ ウミネコ
8. ☑ スズメ
9. ☑ オウム
10. ☑ インコ
11. ☑ 九官鳥
12. ☑ クジャク
13. ☑ ダチョウ
14. ☑ コマドリ
15. ☑ キジ
16. ☑ アヒル

CHAPTER 5. 知識に関する言葉 | 鳥

CHAPTER 5 Knowledge
Birds

1. chicken
2. swallow
3. penguin
4. eagle
5. hawk
6. crow
7. black-tailed gull
8. sparrow
9. parrot
10. parakeet
11. myna bird
12. peacock
13. ostrich
14. robin
15. pheasant
16. duck

CHAPTER 5 知識に関する言葉

色

1. ☑ 黄土色
2. ☑ 黄緑色
3. ☑ 緋色
4. ☑ 群青色
5. ☑ 朱色
6. ☑ 小豆色
7. ☑ 紺色
8. ☑ 肌色
9. ☑ ねずみ色
10. ☑ 褐色
11. ☑ 深紅
12. ☑ 亜麻色
13. ☑ 透明
14. ☑ こげ茶色
15. ☑ 水色
16. ☑ 虹色

CHAPTER 5. 知識に関する言葉 | 色

CHAPTER 5   Knowledge
Colors

1. ☑ ocher
2. ☑ yellowish green
3. ☑ scarlet
4. ☑ ultramarine
5. ☑ vermilion
6. ☑ russet
7. ☑ navy blue
8. ☑ flesh-colored
9. ☑ gray
10. ☑ brown
11. ☑ crimson
12. ☑ flax
13. ☑ transparency
14. ☑ dark brown
15. ☑ sky blue
16. ☑ rainbow colors

CHAPTER 5 知識に関する言葉

植物

1. ☑ さくら
2. ☑ あじさい
3. ☑ つばき
4. ☑ 松
5. ☑ 竹
6. ☑ 梅
7. ☑ 杉
8. ☑ 藤
9. ☑ 彼岸花
10. ☑ たんぽぽ
11. ☑ 朝顔
12. ☑ なでしこ
13. ☑ すずらん
14. ☑ 菜の花
15. ☑ しょうぶ
16. ☑ ききょう

CHAPTER 5. 知識に関する言葉 | 植物

CHAPTER 5 — Knowledge
Plants

1. cherry blossom
2. hydrangea
3. camellia
4. pine
5. bamboo
6. plum
7. Japanese cedar
8. wisteria
9. spider lily
10. dandelion
11. morning glory
12. pink
13. lily of the valley
14. rape blossom
15. iris
16. Chinese bellflower

CHAPTER 5　スケジュール
知識に関する言葉

1. スケジュールを立てる
2. スケジュールを立て直す
3. スケジュールを相談する
4. スケジュールを確認する
5. スケジュールを調整する
6. スケジュールがガラガラ
7. スケジュールに空きがない
8. スケジュールを埋める
9. スケジュールを守る
10. スケジュールどおりに進む
11. スケジュールより進んでいる
12. スケジュールより遅れている
13. スケジュールを勘違いする
14. タイトなスケジュール
15. 余裕のあるスケジュール
16. スケジュール帳

CHAPTER 5. 知識に関する言葉 | スケジュール

CHAPTER 5
Knowledge
Schedules

1. schedule
2. reschedule
3. consult someone about a schedule
4. confirm a schedule
5. adjust a schedule
6. my schedule is blank
7. have no opening in a schedule
8. fill a schedule
9. keep to a schedule
10. be on schedule
11. be ahead of schedule
12. be behind schedule
13. misread a schedule
14. a tight schedule
15. a light schedule
16. appointment book

CHAPTER 6

家に関する言葉
House

炊事、洗濯、掃除などの日々の生活で必ず行うものや、食器や寝具、トイレなどの家の中でよく目にするもの。そういった日々の生活に関係した言葉をまとめました。

House

INDEX

- ●掃除
- ●洗濯
- ●料理 1
- ●料理 2
- ●料理 3
- ●食器
- ●化粧、洗顔
- ●トイレ
- ●車、バイク、自転車
- ●電気
- ●宅配便
- ●寝具
- ●生活
- ●家

CHAPTER 6　家に関する言葉
掃除

1. ☐ 掃除する
2. ☐ 掃除を手伝う
3. ☐ 掃除を怠る
4. ☐ 掃除をあまりしない
5. ☐ 掃除機をかける
6. ☐ 掃除機を取り出す
7. ☐ 掃除機をしまう
8. ☐ 部屋を掃く
9. ☐ 部屋を整頓する
10. ☐ 壁のほこりを落とす
11. ☐ カビを落とす
12. ☐ ほこりをとる
13. ☐ ぞうきん
14. ☐ はたき
15. ☐ ほうき
16. ☐ ちりとり

CHAPTER 6. 家に関する言葉｜掃除

CHAPTER 6
House
Cleaning

1. clean up
2. help someone clean
3. put off cleaning
4. hardly ever cleans
5. vacuum a room
6. get out the vacuum cleaner
7. put away the vacuum cleaner
8. sweep a room
9. tidy up a room
10. dust a wall
11. brush off mold
12. dust off
13. dustcloth
14. duster
15. broom
16. dust pan

CHAPTER 6 家に関する言葉
洗濯

1. ☐ 洗濯する
2. ☐ 洗濯物を洗濯機に放り込む
3. ☐ 洗濯物をかごに入れる
4. ☐ 洗濯物を取り込む
5. ☐ 洗濯物を乾かす
6. ☐ 洗濯物を乾燥機に入れる
7. ☐ 洗い
8. ☐ すすぎ
9. ☐ 脱水
10. ☐ 乾燥
11. ☐ 洗濯洗剤
12. ☐ 柔軟仕上げ剤
13. ☐ 洗濯用ネット
14. ☐ 洗濯ひも
15. ☐ 物干し竿
16. ☐ 全自動洗濯機

CHAPTER 6. 家に関する言葉 | 洗濯

CHAPTER 6
House
Wash the laundry

1. wash
2. put laundry in the washing machine
3. put laundry in a hamper
4. bring in the clothes
5. dry the laundry
6. put laundry in the dryer
7. wash (cycle)
8. rinse (cycle)
9. spin (cycle)
10. dry (cycle)
11. laundry detergent
12. laundry softener
13. laundry net
14. laundry line
15. laundry bar
16. a fully automatic washing machine

CHAPTER 6　家に関する言葉
料理 1

1. ☑ 手抜き料理
2. ☑ 冷凍食品
3. ☑ 電子レンジでチンする
4. ☑ 電子レンジで解凍する
5. ☑ 電子レンジで加熱する
6. ☑ 電子レンジで温める
7. ☑ 煮る
8. ☑ 炊く
9. ☑ 焼く
10. ☑ ゆでる
11. ☑ あえる
12. ☑ 蒸す
13. ☑ まぜる
14. ☑ こねる
15. ☑ だしをとる
16. ☑ 皮をむく

CHAPTER 6. 家に関する言葉 | 料理 1

CHAPTER 6
House
Cooking 1

1. sloppily made food

2. frozen food

3. microwave something

4. defrost something in the microwave

5. heat up something in the microwave

6. warm up something in the microwave

7. simmer

8. cook

9. bake

10. boil

11. dress

12. steam

13. mix

14. knead

15. make soup stock

16. peel

CHAPTER 6 家に関する言葉
料理 2

1. ☐ いちょう切り
2. ☐ みじん切り
3. ☐ 千切り
4. ☐ 短冊切り
5. ☐ 小さじ／大さじ
6. ☐ 1カップ
7. ☐ 塩をひとつまみ
8. ☐ 適量
9. ☐ 電子レンジ
10. ☐ 冷蔵庫
11. ☐ 冷凍庫
12. ☐ 鍋
13. ☐ 蒸し器
14. ☐ おたま
15. ☐ 包丁
16. ☐ 炊飯器

CHAPTER 6. 家に関する言葉 | 料理 2

CHAPTER 6　House
Cooking 2

1. ☑ quarter slice
2. ☑ mince
3. ☑ shredded
4. ☑ strip cut
5. ☑ teaspoon/ tablespoon
6. ☑ 1 cup
7. ☑ a pinch of salt
8. ☑ to taste
9. ☑ microwave
10. ☑ refrigerator
11. ☑ freezer
12. ☑ pot
13. ☑ steamer
14. ☑ ladle
15. ☑ kitchen knife
16. ☑ rice cooker

CHAPTER 6 家に関する言葉
料理 3

1. ☑ ざる
2. ☑ フライパン
3. ☑ まな板
4. ☑ シンク
5. ☑ ふきん
6. ☑ ゴムべら
7. ☑ 泡だて器
8. ☑ ラップ
9. ☑ アルミホイル
10. ☑ オーブン
11. ☑ 食洗機
12. ☑ トースター
13. ☑ やかん
14. ☑ 圧力鍋
15. ☑ コーヒーメーカー
16. ☑ ミキサー

CHAPTER 6. 家に関する言葉 | 料理 3

CHAPTER 6 House
Cooking 3

1. ☑ sieve, strainer
2. ☑ frying pan
3. ☑ cutting board
4. ☑ sink
5. ☑ kitchen towels
6. ☑ rubber spatula
7. ☑ whisk
8. ☑ wrap
9. ☑ aluminum foil
10. ☑ oven
11. ☑ dishwasher
12. ☑ toaster
13. ☑ kettle
14. ☑ pressure cooker
15. ☑ coffee blender
16. ☑ mixer

CHAPTER 6 家に関する言葉
食器

1. ☑ はし
2. ☑ はし置き
3. ☑ お椀
4. ☑ 茶碗
5. ☑ 大皿
6. ☑ 小皿
7. ☑ 重箱
8. ☑ 徳利
9. ☑ おちょこ
10. ☑ 湯飲み
11. ☑ 急須
12. ☑ 土鍋
13. ☑ フォーク
14. ☑ スプーン
15. ☑ ナイフ
16. ☑ マグカップ

CHAPTER 6. 家に関する言葉｜食器

CHAPTER 6
House
Tableware

1. ☑ chopsticks
2. ☑ chopstick rest
3. ☑ bowl
4. ☑ cup
5. ☑ platter
6. ☑ saucer
7. ☑ nest of boxes
8. ☑ liquor bottle
9. ☑ sake cup
10. ☑ teacup
11. ☑ teapot
12. ☑ earthen pot
13. ☑ fork
14. ☑ spoon
15. ☑ knife
16. ☑ mug

CHAPTER 6 家に関する言葉
化粧、洗顔

1. ☑ 乳液
2. ☑ 美容液
3. ☑ 口紅
4. ☑ チーク
5. ☑ 保湿クリーム
6. ☑ 洗顔フォーム
7. ☑ ファンデーション
8. ☑ 日焼け止め
9. ☑ 化粧水
10. ☑ メイク落とし
11. ☑ マスカラ
12. ☑ アイライナー
13. ☑ リップクリーム
14. ☑ シェービングフォーム
15. ☑ カミソリ
16. ☑ 電動カミソリ

CHAPTER 6. 家に関する言葉 | 化粧、洗顔

CHAPTER 6
House
Makeup, facial

1. emulsion fluid
2. serum
3. lipstick
4. cheek rouge
5. moisturizing cream
6. cleansing foam
7. foundation
8. sunblock
9. lotion
10. makeup remover
11. mascara
12. eyeliner
13. lip balm
14. shaving foam
15. razor
16. electric shaver

CHAPTER 6 家に関する言葉
トイレ

1. ☑ トイレに並ぶ
2. ☑ トイレのふたを開ける
3. ☑ トイレのふたをする
4. ☑ トイレを流す
5. ☑ トイレのレバーを押す
6. ☑ トイレを詰まらせる
7. ☑ トイレの水が止まらなくなる
8. ☑ トイレが流れない
9. ☑ トイレットペーパーがなくなる
10. ☑ 公衆トイレ
11. ☑ 有料トイレ
12. ☑ トイレのタンク
13. ☑ トイレの芳香剤
14. ☑ 和式トイレ
15. ☑ 洋式トイレ
16. ☑ ウォシュレット

CHAPTER 6. 家に関する言葉 | トイレ

CHAPTER 6
House
Bathroom

1. line up at the restroom
2. open the toilet lid
3. put down the toilet lid
4. flush the toilet
5. push down on the flush lever
6. clog up the toilet
7. the water won't stop running
8. can't flush the toilet
9. run out of toilet paper
10. public toilet
11. pay bathroom
12. toilet tank
13. toilet deodorant
14. Japanese-style toilet
15. Western-style toilet
16. toilet seat with bidet

CHAPTER 6 家に関する言葉
車、バイク、自転車

1. ☑ 車を路肩に寄せる

2. ☑ 車のワイパーを動かす／止める

3. ☑ ワゴン

4. ☑ レンタカー

5. ☑ シートベルト

6. ☑ 運転席

7. ☑ 助手席

8. ☑ 後部座席

9. ☑ バックミラー

10. ☑ サイドミラー

11. ☑ ママチャリ

12. ☑ マウンテンバイク

13. ☑ カーナビ

14. ☑ ミニバン

15. ☑ 電動自転車

16. ☑ オートバイ

CHAPTER 6. 家に関する言葉｜車、バイク、自転車

CHAPTER 6
House
Cars, motorcycles, bicycles

1. pull the car over to the side of the road
2. turn on/off the windshield wipers
3. station wagon
4. rental car
5. car seat belt
6. driver's seat
7. passenger seat
8. rear seat
9. rear-view mirror
10. side mirror
11. granny bike
12. mountain bike
13. car navigation system
14. minivan
15. electric bicycle
16. motorcycle

CHAPTER 6 家に関する言葉
電気

1. ☑ 電気を消し忘れる
2. ☑ 電気が切れる
3. ☑ 電気を無駄づかいする
4. ☑ ちかちかしている電気
5. ☑ まぶしい電気
6. ☑ 電気温水器
7. ☑ 電気ポット
8. ☑ 白熱灯
9. ☑ 蛍光灯
10. ☑ 裸電球
11. ☑ 乾電池
12. ☑ 単3電池
13. ☑ 単4電池
14. ☑ アルカリ乾電池
15. ☑ マンガン乾電池
16. ☑ コンセント

CHAPTER 6.　家に関する言葉｜電気

CHAPTER 6
House
Electricity

1. forget to turn off the light
2. blackout
3. waste electricity
4. blinking light bulb
5. bright light
6. electric water heater
7. electric pot
8. incandescent light
9. fluorescent light
10. naked light bulb
11. battery
12. AA battery
13. AAA battery
14. alkaline battery
15. manganese dry cell battery
16. outlet

CHAPTER 6　家に関する言葉
宅配便

1. ☑ 荷物を送る
2. ☑ 荷物が届かない
3. ☑ 伝票
4. ☑ 不在票
5. ☑ 最大重量
6. ☑ 日にち指定
7. ☑ 時間指定
8. ☑ 当日便
9. ☑ 代引き
10. ☑ クール便
11. ☑ 壊れ物
12. ☑ 取扱注意
13. ☑ 着払い
14. ☑ 自宅受け取り
15. ☑ コンビニ受け取り
16. ☑ 営業所受け取り

CHAPTER 6. 家に関する言葉 | 宅配便

CHAPTER 6 House
Courier services

1. send a package
2. not arrive
3. invoice
4. absence contact slip
5. maximum weight
6. specified delivery date
7. specified delivery time
8. same-day flight
9. cash on delivery
10. refrigerated delivery
11. fragile
12. handle with care
13. cash on delivery
14. home delivery
15. convenience store delivery
16. customer pick-up

CHAPTER 6 家に関する言葉
寝具

1. ☑ 羽毛布団
2. ☑ ブランケット
3. ☑ シーツ
4. ☑ 枕
5. ☑ 抱き枕
6. ☑ マットレス
7. ☑ 掛け布団
8. ☑ 敷布団
9. ☑ 布団カバー
10. ☑ ベッドメークする
11. ☑ ベッドに潜る
12. ☑ ベッドの上で暴れる
13. ☑ クッションの効いたベッド
14. ☑ 二段ベッド
15. ☑ 寝袋
16. ☑ 空気マット

CHAPTER 6. 家に関する言葉｜寝具

CHAPTER 6　House
Bedding

1 ☑ duvet	9 ☑ quilt cover
2 ☑ blanket	10 ☑ make a bed
3 ☑ sheet	11 ☑ crawl into bed
4 ☑ pillow	12 ☑ keep moving around in bed
5 ☑ cradling pillow	13 ☑ well-cushioned bed
6 ☑ mattress	14 ☑ bunk bed
7 ☑ comforter	15 ☑ sleeping bag
8 ☑ sleeping mat	16 ☑ air mattress

CHAPTER 6 　生活

家に関する言葉

1. ☑ 生活を送る
2. ☑ 生活を楽しむ
3. ☑ 生活を改善する
4. ☑ 生活を立て直す
5. ☑ 生活に苦しむ
6. ☑ 新生活
7. ☑ 結婚生活
8. ☑ 家庭生活
9. ☑ 大学生活
10. ☑ 寮生活
11. ☑ 自堕落な生活
12. ☑ 放蕩な生活
13. ☑ 怠惰な生活
14. ☑ めまぐるしい生活
15. ☑ 放浪生活
16. ☑ 都会生活

CHAPTER 6. 家に関する言葉｜生活

CHAPTER 6
House
Life

1. lead a life
2. enjoy life
3. improve one's life
4. rebuild one's life
5. have a difficult life
6. new life
7. married life
8. family life
9. college life
10. dormitory life
11. sleazy life
12. life of debauchery
13. lazy life
14. hectic life
15. life of wandering
16. urban life

CHAPTER 6 家に関する言葉
家

1. ☑ 和室
2. ☑ 洋室
3. ☑ 玄関
4. ☑ 居間
5. ☑ 畳
6. ☑ 障子
7. ☑ ふすま
8. ☑ 子ども部屋
9. ☑ バルコニー
10. ☑ 洗面所
11. ☑ 浴室
12. ☑ クローゼット
13. ☑ たんす
14. ☑ 押入れ
15. ☑ 下駄箱
16. ☑ 主寝室

CHAPTER 6. 家に関する言葉 | 家

CHAPTER 6 — House

House

1. Japanese-style room
2. Western-style room
3. entrance
4. living room
5. tatami mat
6. shoji screen
7. sliding door
8. children's room
9. balcony
10. washroom
11. bathroom
12. closet
13. chest of drawers
14. closet
15. shoe cupboard
16. master bedroom

CHAPTER 7

街に関する言葉
City

電車、タクシー、バスなどの乗り物や、お店、銀行、神社やお寺など、日本の街でよく見かけるものをまとめました。道を聞かれた時や場所を案内する際に使えます。

City

....

INDEX

- ●お店
- ●コンビニ
- ●買い物
- ●電車
- ●駅、切符
- ●タクシー、バス
- ●信号、道路
- ●学校関連
- ●公共施設
- ●神社、仏閣
- ●銀行

CHAPTER 7　街に関する言葉
お店

1. ☑ 百貨店
2. ☑ ショッピングセンター
3. ☑ アウトレットモール
4. ☑ フードコート
5. ☑ デパ地下
6. ☑ スーパー
7. ☑ 100均
8. ☑ 個人商店
9. ☑ リサイクルショップ
10. ☑ レンタルショップ
11. ☑ キオスク
12. ☑ ホームセンター
13. ☑ 商店街
14. ☑ 地下街
15. ☑ おみやげ店
16. ☑ ドラッグストア

CHAPTER 7. 街に関する言葉 | お店

CHAPTER 7
Towns and cities
Shops

1. department store
2. shopping center
3. outlet mall
4. food court
5. department store basement
6. supermarket
7. 100-yen shop
8. privately owned shop
9. thrift shop
10. rental shop
11. kiosk
12. home center
13. shopping street
14. underground shopping center
15. souvenir shop
16. drugstore

CHAPTER 7 街に関する言葉
コンビニ

1. コンビニに立ち寄る
2. コンビニで買い物する
3. コンビニでコピーを取る
4. コンビニで立ち読みする
5. コンビニで公共料金を払う
6. コンビニでお弁当を買う
7. コンビニで傘を買う
8. 24時間営業のコンビニ
9. 深夜まで営業しているコンビニ
10. 品揃えの豊富なコンビニ
11. 品揃えの悪いコンビニ
12. コンビニの揚げ物
13. コンビニコーヒー
14. コンビニのスイーツ
15. コンビニATM
16. コンビニアルバイト

CHAPTER 7. 街に関する言葉｜コンビニ

CHAPTER 7
Towns and cities
Convenience stores

1. stop by a convenience store
2. shop at a convenience store
3. make a copy at a convenience store
4. stand and read something at a convenience store
5. pay utility bills at a convenience store
6. buy a boxed lunch at a convenience store
7. buy an umbrella at a convenience store
8. 24-hour convenience store
9. late-night convenience store
10. convenience store with almost everything
11. a poor selection convenience store
12. convenience-store fried food
13. convenience-store coffee
14. convenience-store sweets
15. warm up a lunch box
16. work part-time at a convenience store

CHAPTER 7 街に関する言葉
買い物

1. ☐ クレジットカード払い
2. ☐ デビットカード払い
3. ☐ 電子カード払い
4. ☐ 現金払い
5. ☐ おさいふケータイで払う
6. ☐ ポイントをためる
7. ☐ ポイントを使う
8. ☐ 割引券
9. ☐ 30%オフの商品
10. ☐ 両替
11. ☐ おつり
12. ☐ レシート
13. ☐ 領収書
14. ☐ 商品を交換する
15. ☐ 開店セール
16. ☐ レジ

CHAPTER 7. 街に関する言葉｜買い物

CHAPTER 7
Towns and cities
Shopping

1. credit card payment
2. debit card payment
3. electronic card payment
4. cash payment
5. pay with my cell phone
6. save points (on a point card)
7. use my points
8. discount coupon
9. 30-percent discounted item
10. money exchange
11. change
12. receipt
13. receipt
14. replace
15. opening sale
16. cash register

CHAPTER 7 街に関する言葉
電車

1 ☐ 電車に乗る	9 ☐ 特急列車
2 ☐ 電車を降りる	10 ☐ 普通列車
3 ☐ 電車で寝過ごす	11 ☐ 新幹線
4 ☐ 電車のドアに挟まれる	12 ☐ 夜行列車
5 ☐ 快速電車	13 ☐ 満員電車
6 ☐ 通勤電車	14 ☐ 通勤ラッシュ
7 ☐ 通勤快速電車	15 ☐ ガラガラの電車
8 ☐ 急行列車	16 ☐ 地下鉄

223

CHAPTER 7. 街に関する言葉 | 電車

CHAPTER 7
Towns and cities
Train cars

1. get on a train
2. get off a train
3. sleep past my train stop
4. get caught in a train door
5. rapid train
6. commuter train
7. commuter express train
8. express train
9. limited-express train
10. local train
11. Shinkansen
12. overnight train
13. crowded train
14. commuter rush
15. empty train
16. subway
    (イギリスでは tube)

CHAPTER 7 街に関する言葉
駅、切符

1. ☑ 駅で (電車に) 乗り遅れる
2. ☑ 駅で (電車を) 乗り間違える
3. ☑ 始発駅
4. ☑ 終着駅
5. ☑ 通過駅
6. ☑ 改札口
7. ☑ 北/南/東/西口
8. ☑ ホーム
9. ☑ 〜番線のホーム
10. ☑ 〜行きのホーム
11. ☑ 切符を手配する
12. ☑ 切符を改札機に投入する
13. ☑ 乗車券
14. ☑ 指定券
15. ☑ グリーン券
16. ☑ 定期券

CHAPTER 7. 街に関する言葉｜駅、切符

CHAPTER 7
Towns and cities
Train stations and tickets

1. miss a train at a station
2. get on the wrong train at a station
3. the first station on the line
4. the last station on the line
5. non-stop station
6. wicket
7. the north/south/east/west exit
8. platform
9. platform number~
10. the platform for~
11. arrange tickets
12. put a ticket in the wicket gate
13. train/bus/plane ticket
14. reserved-seat ticket
15. first-class ticket
16. commuter pass

CHAPTER 7 街に関する言葉
タクシー、バス

1. ☑ タクシーを捕まえる
2. ☑ タクシーを手配する
3. ☑ 空車
4. ☑ 回送
5. ☑ 割増
6. ☑ タクシー券
7. ☑ カーナビに入力する
8. ☑ バスに乗る
9. ☑ 降車ボタン
10. ☑ バス停
11. ☑ 夜行バス
12. ☑ 高速バス
13. ☑ 発車予定時刻
14. ☑ 回数券
15. ☑ 優先席
16. ☑ 時刻表

CHAPTER 7 Towns and cities
Taxis and busses

1. catch a taxi
2. arrange a taxi
3. empty car
4. out-of-service
5. nighttime fare
6. taxi tickets
7. enter (a location) into the car navigation system
8. catch a bus
9. getting off button
10. bus stop
11. overnight bus
12. expressway bus
13. scheduled time of departure
14. coupon ticket
15. priority seat
16. timetable

CHAPTER 7 街に関する言葉
信号、道路

1. ☑ 赤／黄／青信号
2. ☑ 信号を守る
3. ☑ 信号で止まる
4. ☑ 信号を無視する
5. ☑ 歩道
6. ☑ 高速道路
7. ☑ 一般道
8. ☑ 有料道路
9. ☑ 十字路
10. ☑ T字路
11. ☑ 路地裏
12. ☑ 交差点
13. ☑ 行き止まり
14. ☑ 通行止め
15. ☑ 一方通行
16. ☑ 歩道橋

CHAPTER 7. 街に関する言葉｜信号、道路

CHAPTER 7
Towns and cities
Stoplights and roads

1. red/yellow/green light
2. obey the traffic lights
3. stop at the red light
4. ignore the signal
5. sidewalk
6. expressway
7. local road
8. toll road
9. crossroads
10. T-junction
11. back alley
12. intersection
13. dead end
14. closed road
15. one way (road)
16. footbridge

CHAPTER 7 学校関連

街に関する言葉

1. 学校に遅刻する
2. 学校を早退する
3. 学校をずる休みする
4. 学校を退学する
5. 進級する
6. 留年する
7. 国立大学
8. 私立大学
9. 公立高校
10. 専門学校
11. 中学校
12. 小学校
13. 幼稚園
14. 保育所
15. 塾
16. 予備校

CHAPTER 7. 街に関する言葉 | 学校関連

CHAPTER 7
Towns and cities
Schools

1. ☑ be late for school
2. ☑ leave school early
3. ☑ sluff school
4. ☑ withdraw from school
5. ☑ move up to
6. ☑ get held back
7. ☑ national university
8. ☑ private university
9. ☑ public high school
10. ☑ technical school
11. ☑ junior high school
12. ☑ elementary school
13. ☑ kindergarten
14. ☑ daycare center
15. ☑ cram school
16. ☑ preparatory [prep] school

CHAPTER 7 街に関する言葉
公共施設

1. ☑ 公園
2. ☑ 図書館
3. ☑ 駐輪場
4. ☑ 駐車場
5. ☑ 市役所
6. ☑ 区役所
7. ☑ 町役場
8. ☑ 税務署
9. ☑ 警察署
10. ☑ 派出所
11. ☑ 消防署
12. ☑ 公民館
13. ☑ 保育園
14. ☑ 保健所
15. ☑ 体育館
16. ☑ 庁舎

CHAPTER 7. 街に関する言葉 | 公共施設

CHAPTER 7
Towns and cities
Public facilities

1. park
2. library
3. bicycle-parking space
4. parking garage
5. city hall
6. ward office
7. town hall
8. tax office
9. police station
10. police box
11. fire station
12. civil servant
13. nersery school
14. health care center
15. gymnastic hall
16. government building

CHAPTER 7 街に関する言葉
神社、仏閣

1. ☑ 神社
2. ☑ 仏教
3. ☑ 神道
4. ☑ 鳥居
5. ☑ 社務所
6. ☑ 狛犬
7. ☑ 本殿
8. ☑ 八百万の神
9. ☑ おみくじ
10. ☑ 学業成就のお守り
11. ☑ 家内安全のお守り
12. ☑ お札
13. ☑ 寺院
14. ☑ 仏像
15. ☑ 本堂
16. ☑ さい銭箱

CHAPTER 7.　街に関する言葉｜神社、仏閣

CHAPTER 7
Towns and cities
Shrines and temples

1. shrine
2. Buddhism
3. Shinto
4. torii symbolic gate
5. shrine office
6. a pair of gurdian dogs at a Shinto shirine
7. main shrine
8. a large number of gods
9. paper fortune
10. amulet for academic achievement
11. amulet for home safety
12. good-luck sticker
13. temple
14. Buddha statue
15. main hall
16. offertory box

CHAPTER 7 街に関する言葉
銀行

- [ ] 1 銀行に口座を開く
- [ ] 2 銀行口座を解約する
- [ ] 3 銀行に預金する
- [ ] 4 銀行で振り込む
- [ ] 5 銀行で入金する
- [ ] 6 銀行で金を引き出す
- [ ] 7 銀行で残高を照会する
- [ ] 8 銀行でカードを作る
- [ ] 9 銀行でローンを組む
- [ ] 10 大手銀行
- [ ] 11 都市銀行
- [ ] 12 地方銀行
- [ ] 13 信用金庫
- [ ] 14 普通預金
- [ ] 15 定期預金
- [ ] 16 通帳

CHAPTER 7. 街に関する言葉｜銀行

CHAPTER 7
Towns and cities
Bank

1. ☑ open a bank account
2. ☑ close a bank account
3. ☑ save money in a bank
4. ☑ make a bank transfer
5. ☑ deposit money in a bank
6. ☑ withdraw money from a bank
7. ☑ confirm my account balance
8. ☑ apply for a card at a bank
9. ☑ get a loan from a bank
10. ☑ major bank
11. ☑ city bank
12. ☑ regional bank
13. ☑ credit association
14. ☑ savings account
15. ☑ time-deposit account
16. ☑ bankbook